The Gainesville Sun

A YEAR FOR THE GATORS

FLORIDA GATORS
2006 BCS NATIONAL CHAMPIONS

SP
SPORTS PUBLISHING
L.L.C.

SportsPublishingLLC.com

SportsPublishingLLC.com

Publishers: **Peter L. Bannon and Joseph J. Bannon Sr.**
Senior Managing Editor: **Susan M. Moyer**
Acquisitions Editor: **Noah Amstadter**
Developmental Editor: **Erin Linden-Levy**
Art Director: **Jeff Higgerson**
Cover Design: **Joseph Brumleve**
Book Layout: **Erin Linden-Levy, Doug Hoepker, Laura E. Podeschi and Jeff Higgerson**
Imaging: **Dustin J. Hubbart and Jeff Higgerson**

Publisher: **James E. Doughton**
Executive Editor: **James R. Osteen**
Managing Editor: **Jacalyn Levine**

Front and back cover photos by Doug Finger/The Gainesville Sun.

© 2007 The Gainesville Sun. www.gainesville.com.

ISBN 10: 1-59670-261-3
ISBN 13: 978-1-59670-261-5

CONTENTS

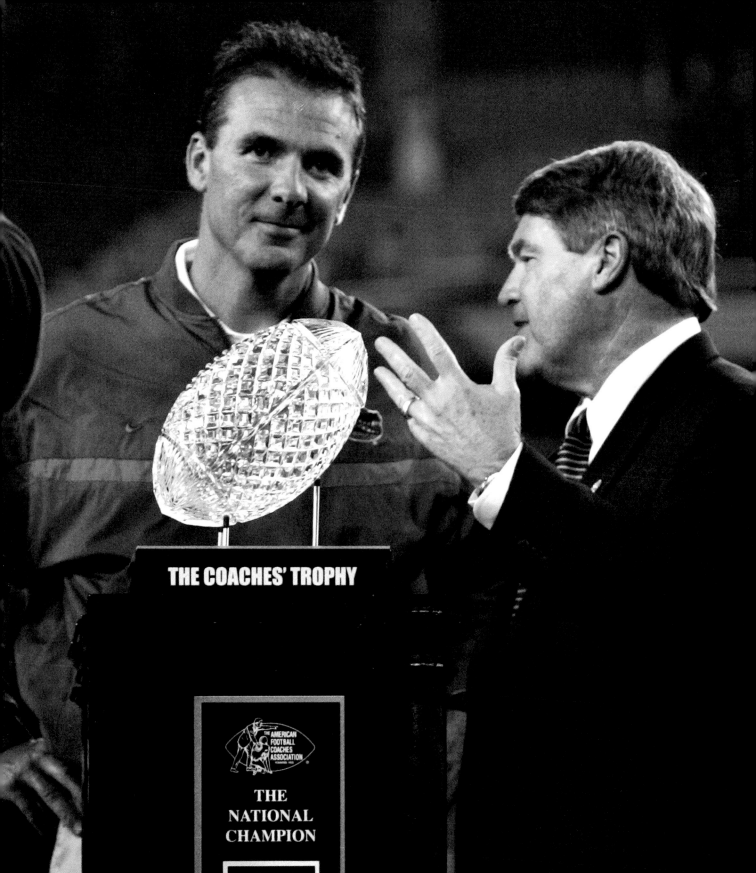

THE COACHES' TROPHY

THE
NATIONAL
CHAMPION

UNIVERSITY OF
FLORIDA
2006

USA TODAY
TOP 25
COACHES' POLL

BOWL
CHAMPIONSHIP
SERIES

INTRODUCTION

As the University of Florida Gators prepared for their 100th anniversary season of football, even some of the most diehard Gator fans looked at the extremely tough 2006 SEC schedule and concluded two or three losses could be seen as a good record and four losses might be realistic.

On sports talks shows, the Gator Nation worried endlessly about the offense—certainly not a mirror image of past Urban Meyer "spread offenses," which rolled up big yardage and the style points to impress voters in the national polls.

Yet, as this remarkable season unfolded, there always seemed like just enough magic moments to snare a victory, despite lapses, frustrations and the omnipresent nail-biting finishes.

Chris Leak, the senior quarterback, teamed with true freshman Tim Tebow and Percy Harvin and some talented receivers to create big plays and score enough points to win.

And the Gator defense and special teams were outstanding, allowing 20 points only three times this season.

Urban Meyer's teams have historically seen major improvement in his second year. But an SEC championship and a 12-1 record with one of the nation's most demanding schedules were an unexpected holiday gift for Gators fans.

And now, a second national championship has made this 100th season even more historic and truly a season to remember.

The sports, news and photography departments of *The Gainesville Sun* provided readers with day-to-day coverage of this incredible season, concluding with the win over the top-ranked Ohio State Buckeyes in Arizona.

We are pleased to bring you the inside story of this remarkable team.

Jim Osteen
Executive Editor
The Gainesville Sun

Florida head coach Urban Meyer is presented with the trophy during the celebration after the Tostitos BCS National Championship. *Doug Finger/The Gainesville Sun*

"I've never been so excited as a fan as I was watching the Gators beat Ohio State for the national championship. It was even sweeter to see them win as an underdog—to see them play and execute so well. I'm very proud of the players and coaches, and proud to be a Gator. What a phenomenal finish to a great season."

—Danny Wuerffel, now serving as the Executive Director of Desire Street Ministries (www.desirestreet.org)

Florida quarterback Chris Leak kisses the national championship trophy.
Tracy Wilcox/The Gainesville Sun

Evolution of UF's Face Will Never Stop

By Pat Dooley, *Sun* sports writer

The faces change.

Not just on the football team. In the stands.

On the couches.

The fans change. Some come and some go. Some just get older. The smile lines are there from 1996, the frown lines from Fourth and Dumb. The hair has grayed but you can't help but wonder how much Lindsay Scott, Shayne Wasden and Warrick Dunn accelerated the shading.

More make-up. More stomach. More headaches.

For 100 years, there have been fans of Florida's football teams. The expectations have changed. It used to be "Wait 'Til Next Year." Then next year came, again and again, until it stopped like a car thrown into park.

Satisfied? Hardly. Those expectations ate at Steve Spurrier, then ate up Ron Zook. Now they are nipping at the heels of Urban Meyer, who has reached back to the past to see the future.

If he reached all the way back, he would see helmetless players without a mascot or school colors. From humble beginnings to the Gator Nation. Talk about a growth spurt.

You think about all of the faces of the players, how they have changed as well. Hair fading, kids growing. Crewcuts, dreadlocks, shaggy dos, sideburns, goatees, beards.

The players find the NFL or other schools or jobs or wasted potential. Most of the coaches are hired to be fired. The fans, man, the fans are in it for the long haul.

What those eyes have seen.

Larry Libertore, bouncing along like a waterbug.

Larry Smith limping into the end zone.

Carlos Alvarez open deep.

The stadium going up and up.

Wayne Peace, Cris Collinsworth, Scot Brantley. The Charley Pell Era. The Spurrier Dynasty.

The memories are burned into

your brain, but they are not what keeps you going, keeps you caring. What keeps you going is that you don't know what the future face will look like.

You don't know who the heroes will be or what play will go down in history as one of the greatest ever.

Those plays, oh, those plays. Above the coaches and players and even the games themselves, it's always about the plays.

They are what you remember.

Reaves-to-Alvarez.

Steve Spurrier's kick.

Ike Hilliard's stop-and-go.

Richard Trapp's dodging the entire Georgia team.

Nat Moore making an FSU defender reach for everything and get nothing.

Cornelius Ingram hauls in a pass during preseason practice.
Tracy Wilcox/The Gainesville Sun

Reggie Nelson (1), Reggie Lewis (22) and head coach Urban Meyer watch practice before the start of the 2006 season.
Tracy Wilcox/The Gainesville Sun

Dick Kirk's run. Jimmy Dunn's run. Emmitt's run.

Wes Chandler against Auburn. Kerwin Bell against Auburn. Reidel Anthony against Auburn.

The Rocket. Big Money. The Freak. Cadillac. Touchdown Tommy. The Cuban Comet. T-Bird. Tiger. Cannonball. Quezzie. C-4. Bubba. Danny Wonderful.

This is a season where all of those plays and players will be remembered, 100 years of Gator football. We've pounded you with it all summer and now it's UF's turn.

But with all of the history and tradition and pomp of the celebra-tion, it's still about what is going to happen this year that will deeply affect the face of Florida football.

Will it be twisted?

Will it be smiling?

Will it be screaming?

For Meyer's Gators?

At Meyer's Gators?

This has a chance to be a feel-good season. The talent is there, if a bit thin in spots, for a special year. It's the 10-year anniversary of the national champions, 40th anniversary of the first of two Heismans. Do you believe in numerology?

This much you know—there will be some plays you'll never forget. There will be results that will stay with you a lifetime. There will be games you keep on your DVR for-ever.

The face of Florida's football pro-gram keeps evolving. From wannabes to been there to wanna be there again. From Bachman to Woodruff to Graves to Spurrier. Now Meyer.

Can it take a step forward

That's why we watch. ◤

Quarterback Chris Leak practices handing off to Mon Williams.
Tracy Wilcox/The Gainesville Sun

Meyer Opens Year Two in a Big-Play Way

By Robbie Andreu, *Sun* sports writer

Year Two is supposed to bring great things. More points and potency on offense. More dominance on defense. More and bigger wins.

This is what everyone has been anticipating because this has been the natural order of progression wherever Urban Meyer has been.

The Meyer blueprint. The Gators and their fans have been eager to dive headfirst into it since that last bead of sweat was wiped off the brow after the Outback Bowl victory over Iowa.

It made the Gators' season opener one of the most anticipated in recent years.

Year Two has finally arrived. But for much of opening night, the Gators looked like they were still living in Year One.

Missed assignments. Missed opportunities. A sluggish, sporadic offense. It looked all too familiar.

The Gators, however, managed to make enough big plays in the second half to turn a close game into a comfortable 34-7 victory before 90,043 at Florida Field.

With each positive play, with each second-half touchdown, Year One seemed to finally start surrendering to Year Two.

"This year, my expectation level is a better performance than what you saw out there," Meyer said. "I know these players and the way they trained. There is an expectation level we'd play better at home in the opener. I was disappointed after the game because I felt we could have played so much better."

Meyer was especially displeased with UF's start. On the third play from scrimmage, true freshman wide receiver Percy Harvin ran a poor route and the result was a Chris Leak interception on the Gators' 28. Two plays later, the Golden Eagles stunned the Gators and silenced the festive crowd with a 6-yard touchdown pass from Jeremy Young to Damion Carter.

It was not the way the Gators envisioned opening Year Two.

"I was very disappointed the way the game started. That's not Florida football," Meyer said. "We had a few games start like that last year. It was extremely disappointing. We can't start the game like that.

"The positive is we dug ourselves out. From that point on we played hard. Last year, I don't know if we would have pulled ourselves out of that hole. We were a frontrunner last year. This is one of the first ones where I saw us dig out of a major hole."

The Gators weren't in very deep in terms of points. But, emotionally, it probably couldn't have been a more deflating start to 2006.

The good news is Leak and the Gators eventually pulled themselves out of their funk.

Fans line the entrance as the Gators take the field for the season opener against Southern Mississippi.
Brian W. Kratzer/The Gainesville Sun

	1st	2nd	3rd	4th	Final
Southern Miss	7	0	0	0	7
Florida	7	7	7	13	34

Scoring Summary

1st

USM: Carter 6-yard pass from Young (McCaleb kick)—3 plays, 28 yards, in 1:09.

UF: Baker 21-yard pass from Leak (Hetland kick)—8 plays, 87 yards, in 3:47.

2nd

UF: Wynn 3-yard run (Hetland kick)—5 plays, 36 yards, in 2:38.

3rd

UF: Cornelius 29-yard pass from Leak (Hetland kick)—8 plays, 71 yards, in 3:32.

4th

UF: Tebow 1-yard run (Wilbur pass failed)—2 plays, 6 yards, in 1:13.

UF: Moore 16-yard pass from Leak (Hetland kick)—7 plays, 82 yards, in 3:11.

Team Statistics

	USM	UF
First Downs	17	21
Net Yards Rushing	119	143
Net Yards Passing	176	248
Passes (Comp-Att-Int)	17-37-3	21-30-1
Total Offense (Plays-Yards)	62-295	59-391
Fumbles-Lost	2-0	1-0
Penalties-Yards	8-64	7-44
Punts-Yards	4-183	3-109
Punt Returns-Yards	0-0	4-39
Kickoff Returns-Yards	2-130	6-367
Interceptions-Yards	1-0	3-35
Fumble Returns-Yards	0-0	0-0
Possession Time	31:47	28:13
Sacks By-Yards	2-13	0-0

Kestahn Moore runs for no yardage on a shuttle pass from Chris Leak during the first quarter.
Tracy Wilcox/The Gainesville Sun

Quarterbacks Tim Tebow (15) and Chris Leak (12) embrace after Tebow's first college touchdown, a 1-yard run in the fourth quarter against Southern Mississippi. *Tracy Wilcox/The Gainesville Sun*

"[Percy Harvin is] one of our most electric players."

—Florida coach Urban Meyer

UF managed to take a 14-7 half-time lead on 21-yard pass from Leak to Baker and a 3-yard TD run by senior tailback DeShawn Wynn.

More spotty play in the third quarter made the crowd even more anxious.

The Gators finally gained some breathing room with a 29-yard TD pass from Leak to Jemalle Cornelius with 4:51 to play in the third quarter for a 21-7 lead. True freshman quarterback Tim Tebow put the game away with a 1-yard touchdown run in the opening minute of the fourth quarter.

Leak ended the night on a positive note, with a 16-yard touchdown pass to tailback Kestahn Moore with 5:30 to play.

When Leak had protection, he was very effective. He finished with 21 completions in 30 attempts for 248 yards and three touchdowns.

"I feel more comfortable (in Year Two)," Leak said. "The coaches gave us a good plan and we went in and executed pretty well."

Like the Gators, Harvin recovered from a shaky start.

He caught three passes for 33 yards and was UF's leading rusher with 58 yards on four carries. He added a big-play element to the offense.

"We played a bunch of freshmen, most notably Percy Harvin," Meyer said. "As you can see, he's one of our most electric players, if not our most electric. He played very well. We're going to try and get him the ball."

Meyer said he also plans to give the ball to Tebow more in the game against Central Florida.

Tebow played only two series, the second coming in the game's closing seconds.

Meyer said Tebow did not play as much as he was supposed to because of the circumstances of the game and the fact he was sick and missed a day of practice earlier in the week.

"He's going to be a great player here," Meyer said. "He's going through some growing pains. He's going to be a terrific player. I'll play him in the first half (against UCF) if he has a good week of practice."

One of the positives to come out of the game was the number of players who appear capable of making plays on offense.

"We've got a bunch of guys who can get the ball in the open field and make plays," Leak said. "We've got to make sure we get completions, keep our drives alive and go down and score."

Another positive was the play of the defense, which shut down USM while the Florida offense was struggling. The Gators limited the Golden Eagles to 119 yards rushing and 295 total yards. The defense also came up with three interceptions, by Reggie Lewis, Reggie Nelson and Tony Joiner.

Leak Nearly Flawless

by Robbie Andreu, *Sun* sports writer

We have been hearing it from Urban Meyer throughout the summer, throughout those sticky, suffocating two-a-days in August.

On a September Saturday night in The Swamp, we saw it.

Chris Leak is a better quarterback, a better leader, than he was a year ago.

Meyer has been saying it over and over and now maybe it's time to start believing that he means it.

In one of the most efficient and productive performances of his Florida career, Leak threw for 352 yards and four touchdowns to spark an offensive onslaught (especially in the second quarter) that buried Central Florida 42-0 before 90,210 at Florida Field. The defense did its part, pitching UF's first shutout in the last 58 games.

Led by a near-flawless performance by Leak and a quick-scoring drive engineered by true freshman quarterback Tim Tebow, Meyer's offense was unstoppable in a game-changing second quarter

that saw the Gators score 27 points in the final 8:14 of the first half.

After a shaky junior season in a new offense, Leak now looks confident and in command. He is even helping produce the offensive game plans during the week.

"It's really neat, Chris Leak comes in on Sunday and Thursday and he actually scripts the offense for us for the first 12 plays of the game," Meyer said. "It's a personnel-driven offense, it's not scheme-driven. (Leak) scripts the plays. That's Chris Leak's offense now.

"Chris had a good day."

It would have been hard to script a better second quarter for the Gators. Leading only 7-0, the Gators went on a scoring tear.

Tailback DeShawn Wynn got things started with an 8-yard touchdown run. It was quickly followed by a 28-yard scoring run by tailback Kestahn Moore and a 10-yard TD pass from Leak to Dallas Baker. Then came the capper—a

25-yard TD strike from Leak to wide receiver Andre Caldwell with only four seconds remaining in the first half.

Suddenly, it was 34-0. Game over.

"The second quarter was dynamic," Meyer said. "In the first quarter we had some young players making significant errors. The positive is the speed on the field has (been) enhanced. I'd have to say we're a faster team than a year ago. I'm proud of the way our young players are stepping up and getting involved."

Leak clearly has more and faster weapons to work with than a year ago.

True freshman wide receiver Percy Harvin had another big night, scoring the game's first touchdown on a 58-yard catch and run midway through the first

Tackle Marcus Thomas, playing in his first game of the season, celebrates in the second quarter.
Tracy Wilcox/The Gainesville Sun

	1st	2nd	3rd	4th	Final
UCF	0	0	0	0	0
Florida	7	27	8	0	42

Scoring Summary

1st
UF: Harvin 58-yard pass from Leak (Hetland kick)—5 plays, 79 yards, in 2:31.

2nd
UF: Wynn 8-yard run (Wilbur pass failed)—9 plays, 79 yards, in 3:28.

UF: Moore 28-yard run (Hetland kick)—5 plays, 77 yards, in 2:24.

UF: Baker 10-yard pass from Leak (Hetland kick)—6 plays, 70 yards, in 1:18.

UF: Caldwell 25-yard pass from Leak (Hetland kick)—2 plays, 35 yards, in 0:34.

3rd
UF: Joiner safety.

UF: Caldwell 8-yard pass from Leak (Nappy kick blocked)—10 plays, 66 yards, in 3:31.

Team Statistics

	UCF	UF
First Downs	11	27
Net Yards Rushing	21	204
Net Yards Passing	132	433
Passes (Comp-Att-Int)	17-36-0	25-38-2
Total Offense (Plays-Yards)	60-153	74-637
Fumbles-Lost	0-0	3-2
Penalties-Yards	6-30	10-71
Punts-Yards	9-345	2-84
Punt Returns-Yards	1-1	5-10
Kickoff Returns-Yards	5-59	2-49
Interceptions-Yards	2-3	0-0
Fumble Returns-Yards	0-0	0-0
Possession Time	27:40	32:20
Sacks By-Yards	0-0	2-15

Freshman wide receiver Percy Harvin breaks a Central
Florida tackle after a pass from quarterback
Chris Leak during the first quarter.
Rob C. Witzel/The Gainesville Sun

Dallas Baker is upended after catching a second-quarter pass from Chris Leak. *Tracy Wilcox/The Gainesville Sun*

quarter. He finished with four receptions for 99 yards and added 11 yards rushing. UF unveiled another potential playmaker from the freshman class Saturday. Wide receiver Jarred Fayson caught a pass and rushed for 28 yards on three carries.

Leak has more options now. He and Tebow completed passes to 11 different receivers, as the Gators amassed 433 yards passing and 637 total yards. Tebow sparked one of the second-quarter TD drives with a 29-yard run.

"I'm real comfortable (in the offense)," Leak said. "Coach Meyer gave me the keys to the offense. It's given me confidence. I try to get around to everybody to see what they like and how they feel about certain plays. I go off that and script the plays with the coaches giving me input.

"I love to spread the ball around to a lot of different guys. If you're spreading it around to so many different people, defenses have to play honest. Our guys did a great job of getting balls and blocking for each other and attacking the defense the way we want to."

As good as Leak and the UF offense were at times, the Florida defense may have been even better.

The Gators pitched a shutout and held the Golden Knights to only 153 total yards, much of them coming in the fourth quarter against the backups. And UF did it without the benefit of a turnover.

"A shutout against a bowl team, they are hard to get," Meyer said. "I thought it was great. The addition (of tackles) Marcus Thomas and Steven Harris (who were suspended from the opener) makes us much more powerful against the run.

"I thought our defense played very well. I'm proud of them. It's hard to get shutouts."

In two games, the defense has given up only one score—a touchdown pass in the opening minutes against Southern Miss that was set up by a Leak interception on the UF 28-yard line.

It's been a very strong two-game run for a defense that came into the season with depth issues at linebacker and in the secondary.

The defense even got involved in the scoring Saturday night, when junior strong safety Tony Joiner nailed UCF tailback Kevin Smith in the end zone for a safety in the third quarter.

UF's other second-half score came on an 8-yard pass from Leak to Caldwell midway through the third quarter.

It was an appropriate ending to a standout night for Leak, who watched Tebow run the offense most of the rest of the way.

"We got into a good rhythm on offense," Leak said. "It's a credit to the coaches doing a good job in letting us know what to expect on the field. Our guys knew where they were supposed to go and the offensive line did an excellent job blocking for me."

Reggie Nelson's interception return for a touchdown against Alabama is only one of his many highlights from the 2006 season.
Doug Finger/The Gainesville Sun

Nelson is Better Than Advertised

By Pat Dooley, *Sun* sports writer

Sometimes the hype is overblown (see: Brock Berlin). Sometimes the stars come from out of the blue (see: Louis Oliver). And then there are times when the recruiting services and flapping lips match up perfectly with the performance of a player.

See: Reggie Nelson.

Just don't go over the middle and expose your ribs.

Nelson was one of those athletes whose legend preceded him and by a long period of time. Unable to attend UF because of grades, his hiatus to junior college almost added to his mystique.

Urban Meyer talked before last season about how that was the name he heard all the time even though Nelson had yet to qualify. When he did, Florida finally had what it hadn't had for a long time.

It's not that there haven't been some good ones playing free safety at Florida through the last 20 years, but not one who can do all of the things Nelson has shown he can do—run, hit, catch, think—and all at high levels.

"He's unbelievable," linebacker Brandon Siler said. "He's probably one of the best football players I've ever seen play, what he can do. He's that fast, and he's that little, but he can hit a 300-pounder and knock him on his butt. We've seen him do it several times. And he's just really explosive. I'm always excited to see Reggie out there."

This is what he was supposed to be when he signed. He was supposed to be the kind of player that would be a Jim Thorpe Award finalist, which he is. He was supposed to combine ball-hawking skills with the ability to destroy opposing receivers physically and emotionally. Which he has.

It just took a while.

But it was worth the wait.

Especially when you can make the argument—and I'm just saying that he's in the discussion—that Nelson is the best free safety ever at Florida.

"He does it all," Meyer said. "He's an energizer. He's a leader. Some of the great ones, I could list a bunch of them. He's that type of player that you just knew where he was at all times. He's a great tackler and he's a great athlete. He can cover and tackle. He could be our punt returner, he's our punt blocker, he blocked two punts. He's just all over the field. ...He's as good a playmaker as I've ever been around."

Nelson says that his teammates have made him better, but it's really the other way around. Because of his speed and instinct, Florida can play a single safety and not worry about anybody going over the top.

"We play one high safety," Meyer said. "The field is 53 yards wide. If you play two safeties, obviously you can cover from sideline to sideline much easier. He has the ability, which not many of these safeties have, he can cover sideline to sideline from the middle. This allows us to play one high. One high now you are able to sink another guy into the box."

So Nelson helps the run defense as well as the pass defense. And then you add in his big plays on special teams.

"This ain't no one-man game," Nelson said. "I've got a great front seven. I've been blessed with a good group of dudes, and I'm just adding on to what they are doing."

Adding, maybe, but affecting, definitely.

In a season full of highlights, you can take your pick.

The obvious ones like the 70-yard interception return against Alabama, the blocked punt against Vanderbilt or the two picks against Tennessee.

Or the subtle ones like the recovery of a teammate's fumble against Alabama, the punt return that got the Gators out of a hole against South Carolina or any one of a number of deep passes that were knocked away.

I asked Florida co-defensive coordinator Charlie Strong for his favorite Nelson play this season. It wasn't an interception or a fumble recovery or a blocked kick.

"The hit against La Fell," Strong said. "It changed the game."

You remember. Game tied at seven, LSU on the move. Deep pass down the east sideline and here comes the Reggie Train, hammering receiver Brandon La Fell as the ball sails into the arms of UF cornerback Ryan Smith.

So many to choose from. Now, this. Against Florida State, a team that will throw two quarterbacks and dozens of passes Nelson's way.

It could be the day he wins the Thorpe and becomes an All-American. In truth, it shouldn't matter. ▲

Electric free safety Reggie Nelson lays a hard hit on Arkansas' Darren McFadden. *Doug Finger/The Gainesville Sun*

Gators Stay Strong Through Deficit

By Robbie Andreu, *Sun* sports writer

Are they tough enough?

Apparently so.

Facing a 17-7 second-half deficit and one of the toughest environments in all of college football in Neyland Stadium, the Florida Gators looked like they were headed for more heartache on the road in the SEC. And more questions about their mental and physical toughness.

But this time they didn't fade. They finished.

"That was one of the finest team efforts I've ever seen," UF coach Urban Meyer said. "I think our offensive coordinator (Dan Mullen) called a hell of a game, especially on that last drive."

Chris Leak threw a 4-yard touchdown pass to Dallas Baker with 1:16 to play in the third quarter to draw the Gators to within six, 20-14.

With 6:30 remaining in the game, Leak and Baker hooked up for the winning score—this time on a 21-yard TD pass to put the Gators up 21-20.

Baker, who was wide open in the flat, raced into the corner of the end zone to give the Gators the lead. And the Florida defense, which did a lot of bending in the second half but did not break, made it hold up.

Following the second Leak-to-Baker touchdown, the Vols drove to the UF 39. But an intentional grounding call against quarterback Erik Ainge pushed UT back. Then on fourth-and-16 from the UF 45, Ainge's pass down the middle of the field was intercepted by junior free safety Reggie Nelson with 2:47 to play on the UF 24.

"I hurt us with the ground call," Ainge said. "Anytime you have fourth-and-16 against a group of athletes like Florida has, it's tough. The percentages are low. I tried to sneak one in there. It's one of those things."

UT never saw the ball again.

On third-and-6 from the 28, tailback DeShawn Wynn picked up a tough six yards for the game-clinching first down.

Wynn came up big all night, rushing for 104 yards on 22 carries. He gave the Gators enough of a running game to take the pressure off of Leak and allow the comeback to occur.

Leak completed 15-of-25 passes for 199 yards and three touchdowns as the Gators produced 22 first downs and 320 total yards. The attacking UF defense held the Vols to minus-11 yards rushing on 23 carries and only 220 total yards.

After falling behind 17-7 early in the third quarter, the Gators appeared headed for another painful SEC road loss.

But unlike a year ago, the Gators proved to be resilient.

Leak threw a 4-yard touchdown pass to Baker with 1:16 left in the third quarter to make it a 17-14 game.

Brandon Siler (40) celebrates behind Vols QB Erik Ainge after forcing him to intentionally ground the pass.
Doug Finger/The Gainesville Sun

	1st	2nd	3rd	4th	Final
Florida	7	0	7	7	21
Tennessee	3	7	7	3	20

Scoring Summary

1st

UF: Cornelius 21-yard pass from Leak (Hetland kick)—7 plays, 63 yards, in 3:46.

UT: Wilhoit 36-yard field goal—6 plays, 30 yards, in 2:11.

2nd

UT: Coker 48-yard pass from Taylor (Wilhoit kick)—4 plays, 64 yards, in 1:54.

3rd

UT: Hardesty 1-yard run (Wilhoit kick)—8 plays, 61 yards, in 3:06.

UF: Baker 4-yard pass from Leak (Hetland kick)—8 plays, 72 yards, in 3:40.

4th

UT: Wilhoit 51-yard field goal—12 plays, 43 yards, in 5:17

UF: Baker 21-yard pass from Leak (Hetland kick)—8 plays, 65 yards, in 4:13.

Team Statistics

	UF	UT
First Downs	22	13
Net Yards Rushing	121	minus-11
Net Yards Passing	199	231
Passes (Comp-Att-Int)	15-25-1	18-33-2
Total Offense (Plays-Yards)	66-320	56-220
Fumbles-Lost	0-0	0-0
Penalties-Yards	9-65	4-34
Punts-Yards	4-172	4-193
Punt Returns-Yards	4-65	1-7
Kickoff Returns-Yards	1-8	4-65
Interceptions-Yards	2-0	1-20
Fumble Returns-Yards	0-0	0-0
Possession Time	35:04	24:56
Sacks By-Yards	2-23	3-32

Brandon James is tripped up by Tennessee punter
Briton Colquitt on a first-quarter punt return.
Doug Finger/The Gainesville Sun

Freshman quarterback Tim Tebow (15) celebrates his run for a first down on the Gators' game-winning drive against Tennessee. *Rob C. Witzel/The Gainesville Sun*

> ## "That was one of the finest team efforts I've ever seen."
> —Florida coach Urban Meyer

The Vols got three of those points back on a 51-yard field goal by James Wilhoit with less than five minutes gone in the fourth quarter.

Early in the game, the Gators certainly didn't resemble a team that had problems playing on the road.

In one of the most efficient drives of the season, the Gators drove 63 yards on their second possession to take a 7-0 lead and silence the huge crowd. The score came on a 21-yard pass from Leak to Jemalle Cornelius, who was wide open in the deep right flat.

The drive featured a little bit of everything and kept UT's aggressive defense off balance. True freshman wide receiver Percy Harvin lined up at tailback and ripped off a 12-yard run, and true freshman Tim Tebow replaced Leak for a play and ran for 11 yards. Tebow's run set the Gators up on the UT 21 and Leak then finished off the drive.

Following a 35-yard punt return by true freshman Brandon James, the Gators were on the UT 49 and in a position to build on their lead. But on first down, Leak threw a pass that was intercepted by cornerback Jonathan Wade and returned 20 yards to near midfield.

A 24-yard pass from Ainge to Robert Meachem put the Vols on the UF 22. But the UF defense held and Wilhoit came on and kicked a 36-yard field goal to make it a 7-3 game late in the first quarter.

The UF offense responded with a long drive, but it produced no points when Chris Hetland was short on a 52-yard field-goal attempt.

Moments later, the Vols came up with a trick play that completely fooled the UF defense and gave UT a 10-7 lead. Wide receiver Lucas Taylor took a handoff from Ainge on an apparent end around, but Taylor pulled up and lofted a pass down the left sideline to a wide-open LaMarcus Coker for a 48-yard touchdown play.

James, a true freshman from St. Augustine, produced the most exciting play of the half when he weaved through the Vols on an 84-yard punt return for an apparent touchdown. But the play was negated by a block in the back.

The Gators had a chance to tie the game in the closing minutes of the first half, but Hetland missed a 47-yard field goal attempt with 1:08 to play.

The Vols seemed to take control of the game early in the second half when tailback Montario Hardesty scored on a 1-yard run to give UT a 17-7 lead.

But the Gators played themselves back into the game to set up the dramatic ending. ◣

Surreal Sights Seen in Swamp

By Robbie Andreu, *Sun* sports writer

Some of the loudest cheers of the night were for made extra points.

Florida fans, who once so embraced the Fun 'n' Gun passing antics of Steve Spurrier, were calling for the running quarterback and booing when he was replaced by the passing quarterback.

A true freshman wide receiver even lined up at quarterback and ran for a first down when the game was on the line in the second half.

Welcome to Surreal Night in The Swamp. What would have really made it surreal would have been a Kentucky win.

But the Florida Gators didn't let things turn quite that strange.

Despite heavy doses of weirdness, the No. 5 Gators provided some normalcy with a strong second half that produced a 26-7 victory over the Wildcats before 90,292.

"It never felt like we were stopped (by UK's defense). We were very much out of sync (in the first half)," UF coach Urban Meyer

said. "I can't explain it until I watch the tape. We were panicking on some plays. We'd run the ball a little bit and then take a shot down the field and the drive would end.

"I was proud of the way our players came out and dominated the second half."

Despite an erratic offensive performance in the first half, the Gators rolled up 514 yards of total offense and had a near-perfect balance (235 yards rushing and 279 yards passing). The UF defense overwhelmed UK in the second half.

After leading only 12-7 at intermission (those 12 points were the result of two touchdowns with both extra points blocked), the Gators dominated the second half.

Tailback Kestahn Moore scored on a 4-yard touchdown midway through the third quarter and the Gators put the game away with a 6-yard TD pass from Chris Leak to Cornelius Ingram with 10:04 remaining in the game.

The positive second half not only created a sense of relief, it also may have produced the first hint of a possible quarterback controversy (at least in the minds of the fans).

Even though Leak threw for 267 yards and two touchdowns, the offense sputtered and stalled through long spells. In the second half, true freshman Tim Tebow entered the game and provided an instant spark with his running ability. Tebow's play created quite a buzz in the stands. When Tebow drove UF inside the 10 in the fourth quarter but was replaced by Leak, the fans booed the decision.

Meyer said after the game that Leak and Tebow will continue to complement one another and give opposing defenses two distinctly different looks.

DeShawn Wynn scores the second Florida touchdown of the night, a 13-yard carry in the second quarter.
Tracy Wilcox/The Gainesville Sun

34

	1st	2nd	3rd	4th	Final
Kentucky	0	7	0	0	7
Florida	6	6	7	7	26

Scoring Summary

1st

UF: Cornelius 33-yard pass from Leak (Hetland kick blocked)—6 plays, 74 yards, in 2:44.

2nd

UK: Grinter 1-yard pass from Woodson (Seiber kick)—8 plays, 66 yards, in 4:19.

UF: Wynn 13-yard run (Hetland kick blocked)—7 plays, 78 yards, in 1:37.

3rd

UF: Moore 4-yard run (Hetland kick)—7 plays, 75 yards, in 2:08.

4th

UF: Ingram 6-yard pass from Leak (Hetland kick)—6 plays, 33 yards, in 2:13.

Team Statistics

	UK	UF
First Downs	17	24
Net Yards Rushing	39	235
Net Yards Passing	210	279
Offense (Comp-Att-Int)	26-38-0	16-28-1
Total Offense (Plays-Yards)	60-249	66-514
Fumbles-Lost	2-0	3-1
Penalties-Yards	10-66	10-71
Punts-Yards	9-334	2-104
Punt Returns-Yards	1-5	3-10
Kickoff Returns-Yards	4-75	2-48
Interceptions-Yards	1-21	0-0
Fumble Returns-Yards	0-0	0-0
Possession Time	33:43	26:17
Sacks By-Yards	3-24	6-37

Dallas Baker gains 20 yards in his second first down in a row in the second quarter against Kentucky.

Tracy Wilcox/The Gainesville Sun

Kentucky's Dicky Lyons Jr. tries to elude tackles from Brandon Siler (40) and Ryan Smith in the third quarter.
Tracy Wilcox/The Gainesville Sun

—Florida quarterback Tim Tebow

"We're just trying to keep them off balance a little bit," Meyer said. "There are certain plays Chris is very good at and some Tim is very good at. Tim is a sparkplug. We've got a good rotation going on in there."

Following their big win in Knoxville a week ago, the Gators were hoping for a nice, comfortable victory back at home against a 23-point underdog. But the Wildcats wouldn't cooperate.

After Leak ended UF's opening possession with a 33-yard touchdown pass to Jemalle Cornelius, it looked like the rout might be on.

It was not.

Andre' Woodson and the UK passing game created fits for the UF defense and the Gators found themselves trailing 7-6 with only 1:54 remaining in the first half after Woodson threw a 1-yard TD pass to fullback Maurice Grinter.

Florida managed to steal back the momentum with a near-flawless touchdown drive engineered by Leak. The two-minute drill was culminated with a 13-yard TD run by tailback DeShawn Wynn with only 22 seconds left in the half. Leak completed five consecutive passes in the drive.

"That was key," Meyer said. "We were dead in the water. That obviously gave us some momentum going into the halftime and gave us a little confidence. Up until that point we were totally out of sync. That drive obviously gave us momentum going into the halftime."

Early in the second half, the Florida defense started hitting and sacking Woodson, and the Gators shut down the UK offense over the final two quarters, limiting the 'Cats to only 65 yards of total offense.

"What I saw was great pressure coming from the edge in the second half and that quarterback didn't have a chance," Meyer said.

Ends Jarvis Moss and Derrick Harvey combined for three sacks in the second half and defensive tackle Ray McDonald had two.

"We kept waiting for Moss and Harvey to do that and they did it tonight," Meyer said.

Meanwhile, some interesting (and somewhat strange) stuff was happening when Florida had the ball. The biggest thing was the presence of Tebow, who generated two impressive drives with his running ability. Tebow finished with 73 yards rushing on six carries.

"Everyone did a nice job of blocking," Tebow said. "All I had to do was some running." ▶

UF Toughs It Out for 5-0 Record

By Robbie Andreu, *Sun* sports writer

There was some talk earlier in the week about payback. But payback does not come easy in the Southeastern Conference. Sometimes it doesn't come at all.

Sometimes it comes down to simply surviving.

That's the situation the Florida Gators faced in the second half against Alabama.

It didn't come down to revenge or payback for last season's embarrassment in Tuscaloosa, Alabama.

It came down to surviving.

And like they did in Knoxville a few weeks ago, the No. 5 Gators toughed it out, made the plays when they had to and rallied in the fourth quarter to pull out a huge SEC win.

Getting big plays from their offensive playmakers—and even more big plays from their defensive playmakers—the Gators managed to slip past the Tide 28-13 before 90,671 emotionally drained fans in The Swamp.

"Thank you to our players. They toughed it out," UF coach Urban Meyer said. "They were challenged at the beginning of the season. They were challenged maybe six, seven or eight thousand times on their toughness. That's two games they've come from behind and won.

"The adrenaline surge that The Swamp gives you assisted, but our guys really toughed it out."

After an awful start, this was a game that could easily have gotten away from the Gators. They trailed 10-0 early in the second quarter and had less than 50 yards of total offense.

But UF gained a much-needed lift and a much-needed score by driving 95 yards for a TD in the closing minutes of the first half. Then, in the second half, the Gators took control with some huge plays on offense and some even bigger plays on defense, the biggest being safety Reggie Nelson's 70-yard interception return for a touchdown that put the Gators up 28-13 with only 4:19 to play in the game.

"That was my first interception for a touchdown," Nelson said. "It was a great feeling getting into the end zone."

It was appropriate that the Gators clinched this victory with a big play on defense.

While the offense was stumbling around in the first half, the defense kept the Gators in the game.

Then, in the fourth quarter, the defense helped win the game.

Leading only 14-13 midway through the quarter, cornerback Ryan Smith intercepted a John Parker Wilson pass on the Tide 34. Smith fumbled the ball, but Nelson came up with a big recovery.

Brian Crum (13) and Reggie Lewis (22) celebrate over Alabama receiver Keith Brown after keeping him to short gain in the second half.
Tracy Wilcox/The Gainesville Sun

	1st	2nd	3rd	4th	Final
Alabama	7	3	0	3	13
Florida	0	7	7	14	28

Scoring Summary

1st

UA: Hall 50-yard fumble recovery (Christensen kick).

2nd

UA: Christensen 21-yard field goal—7 plays, 40 yards, in 2:45.

UF: Tebow 2-yard run (Hetland kick)—12 plays, 95 yards, in 5:28.

3rd

UF: Caldwell 16-yard pass from Leak (Hetland kick)—7 plays, 80 yards, in 2:35.

4th

UA: Christensen 26-yard field goal—12 plays, 54 yards, in 4:52.

UF: Baker 21-yard pass from Leak (Hetland kick)—3 plays, 34 yards, in 1:36.

UF: Nelson 70-yard interception return (Hetland kick).

Team Statistics

	UA	UF
First Downs	20	17
Net Yards Rushing	83	133
Net Yards Passing	240	197
Passes (Comp-Att-Int)	21-40-3	15-21-0
Total Offense (Plays-Yards)	70-323	54-330
Fumbles-Lost	3-0	3-2
Penalties-Yards	5-26	9-53
Punts-Yards	3-107	4-150
Punt Returns-Yards	3-6	1-1
Kickoff Returns-Yards	3-54	2-37
Interceptions-Yards	0-0	3-100
Fumble Returns-Yards	1-50	0-0
Possession Time	29:37	30:23
Sacks By: Number-Yards	1-6	3-33

Quarterback Chris Leak cuts through the Alabama defense for a 45-yard run in the second quarter.
Tracy Wilcox/The Gainesville Sun

In the fourth quarter, wide receiver Dallas Baker pulls in a 9-yard, first-down pass from Chris Leak ahead of defensive back Ramzee Robinson. *Tracy Wilcox/The Gainesville Sun*

"We never got down on ourselves when we were losing. We got back in the game and continued to fight."

—Florida linebacker Earl Everett

Three plays later, quarterback Chris Leak threw a jump ball into the end zone that wide receiver Dallas Baker juggled and turned into a 21-yard TD reception with 6:47 to play.

"We never got down on ourselves when we were losing," senior outside linebacker Earl Everett said. "We got back in the game and continued to fight. We are a different team this year."

When the Gators faced adversity in Tuscaloosa last season, they folded in the first half. This time they held on and played their way back into the lead late in the third quarter and made it hold up with some clutch plays on both sides of the ball.

"Our coaches did a great job of adjusting at halftime," said Leak, who threw for 174 yards and two touchdowns. "And our guys did a good job understanding the adjustments. We kept our composure and made all the necessary adjustments we needed to make."

Leak gave the Gators their first lead of the game with 2:39 to play in the third quarter when he found

Andre Caldwell open in the right flat and Caldwell juked a defender and went 16 yards for a touchdown. Officials reviewed the play to make sure Caldwell did not lose possession of the ball as he dove into the corner of the end zone. After an anxious few minutes, the play was ruled a touchdown and The Swamp erupted with its loudest cheer of the day.

"I was worried about Coach Meyer getting on my butt (if the officials had ruled it a touchback and given the Tide the ball on the 20)," Caldwell said. "I was very relieved."

So was the crowd, which had seen the Gators playing from behind since late in the first quarter when Alabama linebacker Prince Hall scooped up a fumble and returned it 50 yards for a touchdown and a 7-0 Tide lead.

Alabama went up 10-0 early in the second quarter on a 21-yard field goal by Jamie Christensen.

The Tide looked in complete control at that point because the UF offense had done nothing.

"That was an awful first quarter," Meyer said.

The Gators put some much needed make-up on an ugly half with the drive of the day, going 95 yards to finally crack the Tide defense. Leak set the offense up with a 45-yard run to the Alabama 3, then true freshman quarterback Tim Tebow bulled his way into the end zone on third-and-goal from the 2.

"Our guys made plays when they had to," Meyer said. "We were dead in the water. Someone asked me on the field (after the game), if you had to say what was the turning point, it was taking the ball 95 yards against that defense. Chris really mixed it up well and had that big run. He did a nice job."

Once Leak and the offense finally took the lead, the defense took over from there.

"When the offense scored, (junior middle linebacker) Brandon Siler gathered up the defense and said, 'The offense did what they needed to do. It's on us now,'" defensive end Jarvis Moss said. "We stopped up and ended up coming through." ◢

Loss Sparked Change

By Pat Dooley, *Sun* sports writer

It was late and it was only going to get later.

The emotional low point of his first season had come only hours earlier in Baton Rouge, Louisiana, where tears were spilled by players in the locker room and their coach in the dingy interview room.

"I kind of forgot about that," Urban Meyer said.

Nobody else has.

It was a draining day spent trying to get an offense to work.

"Jarvis Herring, who I became very close with. ... When you care about a player and you care about what he's done, to see him—he was a wreck," Meyer said. "His life was ruined there for a minute."

When Herring, a senior safety, broke down after the game, Meyer carried that weight across the hallway where he lost it himself. He now says he learned—especially when the jabs, digs and T-shirts started flying—to take a moment to compose himself before speaking to the media.

But he learned a lot more.

That's why he was up working as October 15 turned into October 16. Meyer called his offensive coaches to his home after the plane landed, grabbed every possible blank canvas he could find including napkins and started working on Florida's new offense.

"We put in a lot of plays that night," he said. "It was a late one. I was grabbing things to draw on.

"It did change. We decided to try to move the chains and play great defense. We were in a tough situation (at LSU). They blitzed us, hit our quarterback a lot. Was (Chris Leak) put in a bad situation? Certainly."

What happened at Tiger Stadium a year ago was a wake-up call of sorts for Meyer. Alabama had humiliated the Gators two weeks earlier, but it wasn't until the LSU game that it became clear that something had to change.

Leak was battered by the blitzing LSU defense all day. He was sacked four times and pressured on almost every throw. There were 30 of them, only 11 which were completed. Florida had 11 first downs for the game and only 206 yards of offense.

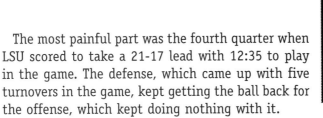

Tracy Wilcox/The Gainesville Sun

The most painful part was the fourth quarter when LSU scored to take a 21-17 lead with 12:35 to play in the game. The defense, which came up with five turnovers in the game, kept getting the ball back for the offense, which kept doing nothing with it.

In Florida's four possessions after LSU took the lead, the Gators had more penalties than first downs and never sniffed the Tigers' side of the field. And a lot of us walked out of the press box not so much impressed with LSU's defense as unimpressed with the Gator offense. It was, in a word, pathetic.

UF kept going to five-receiver formations when there weren't five capable receivers in white jerseys. Not only was it easy for the Tigers to cover Kyle Morgan and Gavin Dickey—sometimes with a single defender—it freed them up to blitz.

The result was a Florida offense that looked as if it was going against a defense with 13 or 14 players on the field. The crowd consumed every negative play for Florida and spit it back out as new energy.

It made for a depressed flight home and a late night for the coaches.

Meyer and his staff not only put some new running plays into the offense that night, they also put fullback Billy Latsko back into the game plan and worked on leaving a tight end in to block. The hybrid offense had been re-worked again and the Gators spent the bye week installing the new stuff.

What has followed has been a very nice run for Meyer and the Gators. Since that miserable day in Baton Rouge, Florida has won nine of 10 games including wins over Georgia, FSU, Iowa, Tennessee and Alabama. The offense has changed again with the arrival of more playmakers, but some of the elements that were introduced during that late night last October are still part of the system.

A lot has changed. Maybe it took a loss that painful to bring the team together in Meyer's first season.

"It was a pretty sad atmosphere," said receiver Jemalle Cornelius. "You could tell the team was hurting."

So was the coach. The Gator Nation found itself fragmented again. The grousing was deafening.

It has eased up since, even though there are certainly still concerns about Florida's offense heading into the LSU game. Because one thing hasn't changed in a year—LSU's defense is really good. ▰

SEC Win Highlights Gators' Solidarity

By Robbie Andreu, *Sun* sports writer

A year ago in Baton Rouge, Louisiana, the tears flowed in the losing Florida locker room.

After this year's game with LSU in The Swamp, there were giant Gator grins all around.

The Gators, who were struggling with this team thing at this stage in Urban Meyer's first season, have clearly evolved into a strong, united front in Year Two.

They have become a team.

In front of 90,714 fans and a national television audience, the Gators produced the working and breathing definition of a team win with their 23-10 victory over the Tigers.

"The hard work this team has put together. ... We do everything together," senior quarterback Chris Leak said. "That's what being a great team is all about. That's what great teams do. They come together and play a strong four quarters against a good team and come up with the victory."

This might go down as one of the great team victories in school history—and certainly the biggest in the infant stages of the Meyer era.

The Gators won with defense—intercepting three passes and coming up with two fumble recoveries.

They won with special teams—blocking a punt and producing a safety on the second-half kickoff.

They won with offense—true freshman quarterback Tim Tebow producing all three touchdowns, running for one and throwing for two.

They won with a little guile and a lot of guts.

They won as a team—wiping out the painful memory of last year's 21-17 loss at LSU.

"Today was a great day for Florida football," Meyer said. "This is one of the best environments that I've ever been a part of. I'll put this against anyone in America after today."

The defining moments in this game were condensed to the clos-

ing minutes of the first half and the opening minutes of the second.

"Lou Holtz always tells me that the last five minutes of the first half and the first five minutes of the second half determine the outcome of the game," Meyer said. "If you had to say what was the checkmate point today, it was the end of the first half and the last five minutes of the second half."

Late in the first half, with the score tied 7-all, LSU appeared to take the lead with a 10-yard touchdown run by fullback Jacob Hester. But Hester was ruled down inside the 1 and a review of the play resulted in the call standing. On the next snap, LSU quarterback JaMarcus Russell fumbled and the ball was recovered by UF middle linebacker Brandon Siler.

QB Tim Tebow (15) celebrates a gain in the first quarter. Tebow scored a few minutes later on a 1-yard run.
Doug Finger/The Gainesville Sun

	1st	2nd	3rd	4th	Final
LSU	**7**	**0**	**0**	**3**	**10**
Florida	**7**	**7**	**9**	**0**	**23**

Scoring Summary

1st

LSU: Hester 2-yard pass from Russell (David kick)—9 plays, 73 yards, in 4:38.

UF: Tebow 1-yard run (Hetland kick)—6 plays, 19 yards, in 3:38.

2nd

UF: Casey 1-yard pass from Tebow (Hetland kick)—9 plays, 72 yards, in 2:49.

3rd

UF: McCollum safety.

UF: Murphy 35-yard pass from Tebow (Hetland kick)—5 plays, 67 yards, in 2:41

4th

LSU: David 45-yard field goal—12 plays, 61 yards, in 4:04.

Team Statistics

	LSU	UF
First Downs	22	14
Net Yards Rushing	90	97
Net Yards Passing	228	191
Passes (Comp-Att-Int)	24-41-3	19-28-1
Total Offense Yards	66-318	60-288
Fumbles-Lost	3-2	3-1
Penalties-Yards	5-30	14-102
Punts-Yards	2-27	5-204
Punt Returns-Yards	3-minus-10	1-6
Kickoff Returns-Yards	4-65	2-36
Interceptions-Yards	1-0	3-13
Fumble Returns-Yards	0-0	0-0
Possession Time	27:25	32:35
Sacks By-Yards	1-9	1-1

Jamalle Cornelius sizes up his LSU defender and makes a 9-yard gain. *Tracy Wilcox/The Gainesville Sun*

Lutrell Alford runs to the sideline to celebrate with his teammates after recovering a fumbled LSU punt return.
Brian W. Kratzer/The Gainesville Sun

A few minutes later, the Gators took the lead.

Following an interception by UF cornerback Ryan Smith, the Gators drove 72 yards to take a 14-7 lead with only 22 seconds left in the half. The score came on a jump pass from Tebow, UF's running quarterback, to tight end Tate Casey.

Tebow, who had scored UF's first touchdown with a 1-yard run, faked like he was running into the middle of the line and then popped up and found a stumbling Casey wide open in the back of the end zone.

"I sort of floated one in the lane," Tebow said. "Tate Casey did a nice job of adjusting to the ball."

The momentum generated by the late score carried over to the second half.

On the second-half kickoff, LSU return man Early Doucet dropped the ball and then was nailed by UF true freshman wide receiver Riley Cooper as he was picking up the ball. Cooper's hit knocked the ball free and it rolled into the end zone, where the Tigers recovered it for a safety and a 16-7 UF lead.

"He was juggling it and I had an opportunity to hit him a big lick and I did," Cooper said. "I put it into another gear and put a lick on him.

"It gave us a lot of momentum."

And the Gators embraced it.

UF received the ball on their own 34 following LSU's kickoff and quickly drove for another touchdown. The score came on a 35-yard pass from Tebow to sophomore wide receiver Louis Murphy. Like he did on his TD pass to Casey, Tebow faked like he was going to run on the second-and-1 play, but then pulled up and launched a pass to a wide-open Murphy for the score.

"We made it look like a run and we were hoping they (the LSU secondary) would bite and they bit," Tebow said.

The touchdown gave the Gators a 23-7 lead and a big-play UF defense made it hold up.

Although Russell and the LSU passing game had the Tigers on the move for most of the remainder of the game, the Gators came up with two big interceptions to seal the win—one by Smith and the game-clincher by strong safety Tony Joiner in the end zone with 3:17 left to play in the game.

"We made mistakes in a number of spots," LSU coach Les Miles said. "We're a good football team, but we didn't play like it today and we're all disappointed."

There was no disappointment in the Florida locker room, where the Gators were celebrating their victory.

"This was a very special and emotional moment for us seniors," said Leak, who completed 17 of 26 passes for 155 yards. "We're going to remember this for the rest of our lives. It is special being a Gator. To beat a great team like LSU means a lot." ◣

Miscues Prove Too Costly

By Robbie Andreu, *Sun* sports writer

Florida's opportunity to take command of the SEC's Eastern Division slipped out of the Gators' grasp at Jordan-Hare Stadium.

Literally.

First out of the hands of punter Eric Wilbur early in the third quarter. Then out of the hand of quarterback Chris Leak in the fourth quarter.

Wilbur's dropped snap turned into a quick Auburn touchdown in the opening minutes of the second half to give Auburn an 18-17 lead, and the Tigers made it hold up for a 27-17 victory before a fanatical crowd of 87,451.

"Right now, we're down. We let this one slip away," UF senior cornerback Reggie Lewis said.

The Gators still hold the lead in the SEC East because of the tie-breaker with Tennessee, which UF defeated a month ago.

"We've got to get cleaned up and get home," UF coach Urban Meyer said. "We've got to protect our first-place standing in the SEC (against Georgia in two weeks)."

The game-winning score came early in the second half, when Wilbur dropped James Smith's snap, then lost the ball to Tre Smith, who returned it 15 yards for a touchdown to give the Tigers a 1-point lead.

Auburn added a touchdown on the last play of the game when Patrick Lee scooped up a UF fumble on a desperation play and returned it 25 yards for the score.

Trailing 18-17 with less than 10 minutes remaining in the game, the Gators had a chance to take the lead. But on third-and-2 from the Auburn 6-yard line, Leak was pressured while attempting a pass and the ball slipped out of his hand and was picked up and returned 22 yards by linebacker Tray Blackmon.

Meyer challenged the play, hoping replays would show Leak's arm was going forward and it was an incomplete pass. But after review, the play stood as called on the field even though it appeared Leak's arm was moving forward.

Leak and the Gators had another chance to make a comeback after Auburn's John Vaughn missed a 45-yard field goal with 3:16 left in the game.

But on UF's first play from the 29, Leak was pressured and threw a floater over the middle that was intercepted by Eric Brock and returned 26 yards to the UF 28. That turnover set up a 39-yard field goal by Vaughn with 32 seconds to play to give the Tigers a 21-17 lead.

"Where is my toilet paper?" Auburn coach Tommy Tuberville said. "I'm going to Toomer's Corner. What a game. Good gosh.

"What a difference a half will make for a defense. We couldn't slow them down in the first half,

A disappointed Chris Leak and his teammates leave the field following their 27-17 loss to Auburn.
Doug Finger/The Gainesville Sun

54

	1st	2nd	3rd	4th	Final
Florida	3	14	0	0	17
Auburn	3	8	7	9	27

Scoring Summary

1st

AU: Vaughn 22-yard field goal—13 plays, 85 yards, in 6:00.

UF: Hetland 22-yard field goal—8 plays, 75 yards, in 4:39.

2nd

UF: Baker 15-yard pass from Leak (Hetland kick)—8 plays, 69 yards, in 3:12.

AU: Team safety.

AU: Vaughn 31-yard field goal—11 plays, 50 yards, in 5:16.

UF: Tebow 16-yard run (Hetland kick)—3 plays, 80 yards, in 0:48.

AU: Vaughn 34-yard field goal—9 plays, 55 yards, in 3:40.

3rd

AU: Smith 15-yard blocked punt return (Vaughn kick).

4th

AU: Vaughn 39-yard field goal—4 plays, 6 yards, in 2:26.

AU: Lee 20-yard fumble recovery.

Team Statistics

	UF	AU
First Downs	18	19
Net Yards Rushing	171	133
Net Yards Passing	108	182
Passes (Comp-Att-Int)	9-17-1	18-27-0
Total Offense (Plays-Yards)	45-279	67-315
Fumbles-Lost	3-2	2-1
Penalties-Yards	5-33	4-40
Punts-Yards	3-92	3-112
Punt Returns-Yards	1-8	1-25
Kickoff Returns-Yards	0-0	5-124
Interceptions-Yards	0-0	1-26
Fumble Returns-Yards	0-0	2-42
Possession Time	23:17	36:43
Sacks By-Yards	5-33	3-25

Earl Everett breaks up a first-quarter touchdown pass to Auburn's Rodgeriqus Smith in the end zone.
Doug Finger/The Gainesville Sun

Tony Joiner (19) hammers the Auburn ball carrier, forcing a turnover in the second quarter. *Brian W. Kratzer/The Gainesville Sun*

"We let this one slip away."

—Florida cornerback Reggie Lewis

and they couldn't move it in the second half."

Auburn added the final score on the last play of the game when wide receiver Jarred Fayson's lateral to Leak hit the ground and was picked up and returned for a touchdown.

The Gators had to stomach the loss even though the defense did not give up a touchdown. The touchdowns by Smith and Lee and a career-high four field goals by Vaughn were the difference.

It was a tough night for Leak, who threw for only 108 yards and had the two turnovers on consecutive plays in the fourth quarter. The Gators were held to only 279 yards of total offense, while Auburn's balanced attack produced 315.

As they have for so much of the season, the Gators found themselves playing from behind after Auburn took the opening kickoff and drove 85 yards on 13 plays, leading to a 22-yard field goal by Vaughn with six minutes gone in the game.

The big play on the drive was a 24-yard pass from Brandon Cox to fullback Carl Stewart that put the Tigers on the 4-yard line.

The Florida offense had an immediate response.

On the strength of tailback DeShawn Wynn's runs and a 20-yard dash by true freshman wide receiver Percy Harvin, the Gators drove inside the Auburn 5.

After Wynn was nailed for a 3-yard loss on third-and-1 from the 3, Chris Hetland came on and kicked a 23-yard field goal, giving UF its first field goal of the season and tying the game 3-3.

The Gators snagged the momentum and the lead on their next possession after the defense forced a three-and-out.

UF drove inside the AU 20, the march spurred by a 16-yard pass from Leak to Andre Caldwell and a 12-yard pass from Leak to No. 2 tailback Kesthan Moore.

On second-and-10 from the 15, Leak lofted a pass into the left corner of the end zone and Dallas Baker snagged it to give the Gators a 10-3 lead with less than a minute gone in the second quarter.

Auburn's Tristan Davis returned the ensuing kickoff 63 yards to the UF 38.

On a first-down pass from the 17, Cox threw to a wide-open Tommy Trott, but he was stripped of the ball and defensive end Derrick Harvey recovered the fumble on the UF 3.

On UF's first offensive play, guard Jim Tartt was called for holding in the end zone for a safety, cutting the UF lead to 10-5.

The Gators had to kick to Auburn and the Tigers were right back in UF territory, where they had to settle for a Vaughn 31-yard field goal to make it 10-8.

Auburn's momentum did not last long.

The Gators responded with an 80-yard touchdown drive in only three plays to give UF a 17-8 lead.

Harvin ran for eight yards on first down, then for 35 on the second. Freshman QB Tim Tebow ran 16 yards into the end zone on his only play of the half.

Auburn made it a 17-11 game at the half with a 34-yard field goal by Vaughn with 29 seconds remaining. ▶

Florida quarterback Chris Leak celebrates a touchdown pass to Andre Caldwell during the Georgia game.
Tracy Wilcox/The Gainesville Sun

Leak's Legacy

By Pat Dooley, *Sun* sports writer

You can criticize his decisions, boo him at home, rip him for sliding short of first downs and want more of the shiny new toy named Tim Tebow.

But you have to say this about Florida quarterback Chris Leak.

He gets Florida-Georgia.

He gets how important it is, how big it is, how exciting it is. He gets the tradition, the color, the sounds, the smells. It's a game he circles on his mental calendar.

"Going to the game is an experience like no other," he said. "The atmosphere is exciting. You get really excited for your family because you know how much they are going to enjoy the atmosphere.

"It's a very emotional game for us players, just the atmosphere. It's a game that you really enjoy playing."

He gets Florida-Georgia. The way he has played has shown it.

In three games as Florida's starting quarterback, Leak is 2-1 and we'll always wonder if that record wouldn't be 3-0 if Leak and his teammates hadn't had their coach pulled out from under them five days before the 2004 game.

His numbers against Georgia are impressive—50-of-77 for 590 yards and four touchdowns, plus last year's rushing touchdown. Most importantly, he has never thrown an interception against the Bulldogs.

And now this, his final shot, his last game in the big rivalry.

With his legacy on the line.

Let's face it, a loss to Georgia probably means that Florida will not be playing in Atlanta and that means Leak will have spent four years at Florida without a ring but with a nice collection of Outback Bowl windbreakers.

But win this game and the next two against Vandy and South Carolina and Leak has returned Florida to the promised land. You know the one with a 30313 zip code.

And that would be his legacy—the guy who quarterbacked Florida back to the SEC Championship Game. And the guy who beat Georgia three times.

That's why Florida needs to place the game in Leak's hands.

I'm not saying that you chain Tebow to the bench. I'm just saying that this game needs to be up to the guy with the most on the line.

He has shown he can handle it, the atmosphere and the heavy aura around this game. I know, his last few snaps against Auburn were a disaster, but he's a senior with big-game experience and four years as a starter going against a team in disarray with a quarterback making his fourth start.

This needs to be Leak's game. Florida has a bunch of weapons and the best way to get them the ball in open space is to have Leak toss it to them.

I'm sure the offensive coaches appreciate my advice on this issue, but it seems to me that if you have all of this talent at wide receiver and you're playing your biggest game of the season and you have a quarterback who has a history of playing well in the game, well, it seems like it would make sense to chuck it around a little bit.

Against Auburn, Leak threw only 13 passes before the desperation tosses in the final 31 seconds and I know that Florida having only 45 plays had a lot to do with it.

But I also know that no player should affect this Florida-Georgia game more than Florida's starting quarterback.

"That's our plan and that's really been our plan all year," Urban Meyer said. "Surely we are going to do anything we need to do to have success, but that's the plan."

Just don't out-think yourselves. And don't call me Shirley.

"He has had success in this game. He knows this game," Meyer said. "We expect him to play very well in this game."

He should. It's his last shot at the Bulldogs. It could be his last shot at a ring. It should be his game to win or lose. ▲

Chris Leak launches a pass to DeShawn Wynn before taking a heavy hit during the fourth quarter against Georgia.
Tracy Wilcox/The Gainesville Sun

Defense, Suspense

By Robbie Andreu, *Sun* sports writer

Urban Meyer stood at the podium underneath Alltel Stadium looking and sounding like the losing coach in the Florida-Georgia game.

He was bemoaning an offense that went stagnant in the second half and was visibly distraught over a rash of penalties, turnovers and other assorted offensive blunders that put his team on the brink of self-destruction.

He was Mr. Negative—and the No. 9 Gators had just beaten the Bulldogs 21-14 before 84,572 to move to 7-1 and take command of the SEC's Eastern Division race.

"My wife is going to smack me in the mouth when I get home for complaining about this," Meyer said.

Meyer could not help himself because the Gators nearly let this one slip away after leading 21-0 early in the second half and having to hang on for the victory in the closing minutes.

"We've got a lot of work to do and we're going to start immediately. We're going to start tonight," he said. "We're going to get this right. We have a lot of issues."

Finally, Meyer lightened up when a writer put things in perspective for the head coach:

"Despite the concerns on offense, your team remains in position for some really nice things if it can play well down the stretch. Southern Cal lost today. You're moving up (in the BCS Standings), you're in the mix (for the SEC championship and possibly the national title)."

That comment brought a winning smile to Meyer's face.

"I appreciate that," Meyer said. "I feel better now. For the first time, you guys have cheered me up. I appreciate that."

Despite all that went wrong (mostly with the offense) in the second half, the Gators won the game and now are two victories away (against Vanderbilt on the road and South Carolina at home) from winning UF's first division title since 2000. The win, coupled with the Trojans' loss, has the Gators inching back into contention in the national title hunt as well.

"We are officially playing for the SEC East championship now," Meyer said.

And, for the Gators, that feels good no matter how bad this performance went against Georgia at times.

"It feels good to control your own destiny," senior outside linebacker Earl Everett said. "We don't need to depend on another team doing something for us like the past few years. It's in our hands."

It almost escaped from their grasp against Georgia.

Two second-half turnovers (a Chris Leak interception and a Tim

QB Tim Tebow scrambles for a few yards during the first half of the UGA game. *Tracy Wilcox/The Gainesville Sun*

	1st	2nd	3rd	4th	Final
Florida	7	7	7	0	21
Georgia	0	0	7	7	14

Scoring Summary

1st

UF: Caldwell 12-yard run (Hetland kick)—9 plays, 62 yards, in 5:49.

2nd

UF: Caldwell 40-yard pass from Leak (Hetland kick)—1 play, 40 yards, in 0:33.

3rd

UF: McDonald 9-yard fumble recovery (Hetland kick).

UGA: Stafford 13-yard run (Bailey kick)—6 plays, 52 yards, in 2:17.

4th

UGA: Lumpkin 8-yard run (Bailey kick)—3 plays, 14 yards, in 0:54.

Team Statistics

	UF	UGA
First Downs	15	14
Net Yards Rushing	156	64
Net Yards Passing	163	151
Passes (Comp-Att-Int)	14-28-1	13-33-2
Total Offense (Plays-Yards)	63-319	59-215
Fumbles-Lost	3-1	3-3
Penalties-Yards	10-75	6-50
Punts-Yards	6-271	7-272
Punt Returns-Yards	5-46	2-4
Kickoff Returns-Yards	3-61	2-30
Interceptions-Yards	2-0	1-0
Fumble Returns-Yards	1-9	0-0
Possession Time	33:58	25:30
Sacks By-Yards	4-21	0-0

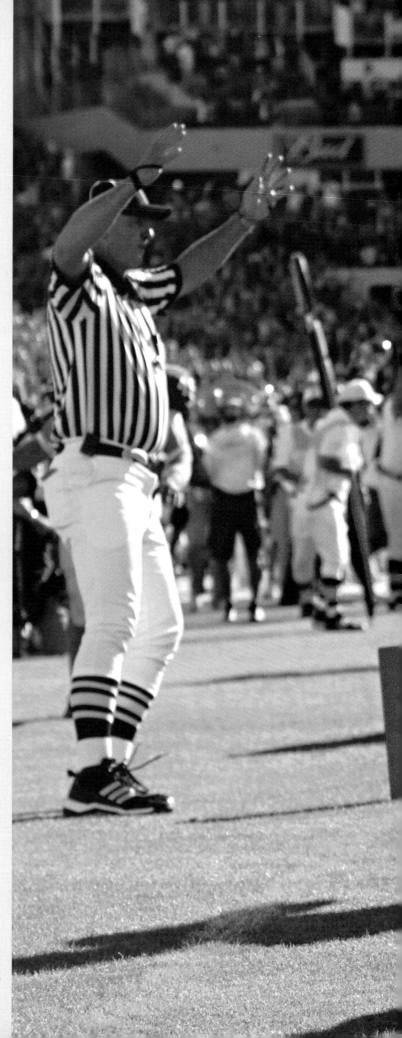

Florida's Brandon James makes it into the end zone in the second quarter, but the touchdown was called back. *Doug Finger/The Gainesville Sun*

The Florida Gators sing to fans after defeating the University of Georgia in Jacksonville. *Doug Finger/The Gainesville Sun*

Tebow fumble) led to two Georgia touchdowns, and the Gators suddenly found themselves leading only 21-14 after tailback Kregg Lumpkin scored on a 9-yard run with 8:17 left in the game.

The UF defense, which dominated for most of the day, made the lead hold up, and the offense did its part in the closing seconds when DeShawn Wynn ran for six yards on third-and-four from the UF 46 that allowed the Gators to run out the final 90 seconds.

The final outcome softened some of the Florida negatives—and there were plenty.

A block in the back penalty wiped out a 66-yard punt return for a touchdown by true freshman Brandon James in the first half.

In the second half, the offense sputtered and stalled, and placekicker Chris Hetland missed two field goals (39 and 42 yards) that could have put the game out of reach.

The Gators also killed themselves with 10 penalties in the game.

Perhaps the biggest negative was the inept performance of the offense in the second half. For the second game in a row, the UF offense was shut out in the second half.

"We'll just have to sit down and watch the film and figure it out," Tebow said. "We'll just work it out and try to execute better. We have to buckle down and fix it."

The offense would offer many thanks to the Florida defense after this one.

The Gators came up with four turnovers—including one for a touchdown on the first offensive play of the second half—and held the Bulldogs to 64 yards rushing and 215 total yards.

"Thank God for great defense," Meyer said. "That was a great effort by our defense. They held a talented Georgia team and a young quarterback (Matthew Stafford) who is going to be tremendous to only 215 yards of offense. Our defense played very hard tonight."

The UF offense started strong Saturday but then self-destructed in the second half.

Florida scored on the game's opening possession on a 12-yard run by junior wide receiver Andre Caldwell.

The Gators went up 14-0 with a 40-yard pass from Leak to Caldwell with 9:37 left to play in the second quarter.

On the first offensive play of the second half, Lumpkin was stripped of the ball by end Derrick Harvey and UF defensive tackle Ray McDonald returned it nine yards for a touchdown. At that point, it was 21-0 and it appeared Florida was heading for an easy victory.

It didn't happen that way. Turnovers gave the momentum to the 'Dogs in the second half and they got right back into the game.

"I don't feel good about this," Georgia coach Mark Richt said. "I don't enjoy losing to the Gators. But I will say this, when most teams would lie down and die, this team didn't. We've got some guys with great character. I'm proud of them and proud to be a Bulldog."

Despite the shaky second half, it's good to be a Gator, too. The division title is within reach.

"It hasn't happened in a long time," said Caldwell, who accounted for 116 total yards and both offensive touchdowns. "It feels good that we might be playing for a championship. We have a lot of improvement to make, though we'll go week by week." ▲

UF Holds On,
Gets Assist from LSU

By Robbie Andreu, *Sun* sports writer

It wasn't perfect or pretty. Not even close. But, it was a win—and it helped turn this into a November to remember for the Florida Gators.

The Gators did what they had to do. They controlled what they could control. Then they sat back and watched themselves become SEC Eastern Division champions for the first time since 2000 when LSU pulled out a last-second victory over Tennessee in Knoxville a few hours later.

"I'm happy for our players, coaches and the Gator Nation," Florida coach Urban Meyer said. "We've got a great group of people who are invested in the program. Getting to Atlanta was certainly one of our goals but we still have some work ahead of us."

After a memorable day in Tennessee for Florida, the Gators are heading to Atlanta for the December 2 SEC Championship Game against the winner of the West.

"That hasn't happened in a long time around here," junior wide receiver Andre Caldwell said. "To accomplish something like that, it's a big statement for Florida football."

The No. 7 Gators survived a late Vanderbilt scare and hung on in the final minutes to gain a 25-19 victory before 38,134 to move to 8-1 for the first time since 2000.

That victory put the Gators an LSU victory away from the division title.

"We are going to get on the plane and we are big LSU fans right now," Meyer said in his postgame news conference. "LSU is a very talented team by the way."

A few hours later, the Tigers made the Gators big winners for the second time by eliminating Tennessee (and everyone else in the Eastern Division) with their 28-24 victory in Neyland Stadium.

The Gators now will not have to beat former coach Steve Spurrier in The Swamp to win the SEC. But

the game is still huge for UF's national title chances, which remain very much alive.

The Gators didn't play like champions, but that's what they were at the end of the day.

Florida's shaky play against the Commodores became almost insignificant in what became the brightest day in Florida football since the Gators won the conference title in 2000.

At times, it appeared the Gators were close to having a breakout game offensively, especially in the downfield passing game.

But the breakout didn't come. Chris Leak threw for 237 yards and a touchdown, but his good work lost some of its shine with three interceptions, two of which killed scoring chances.

Gators QB Chris Leak takes his time in the pocket as he looks past the Vanderbilt defense for a receiver.
Tracy Wilcox/The Gainesville Sun

70

	1st	2nd	3rd	4th	Final
Florida	8	7	10	0	25
Vanderbilt	6	0	0	13	19

Scoring Summary

1st

UF: Leak 4-yard run (Casey pass from Rowley)—2 plays, 6 yards, in 0:52.

VU: Jackson-Garr 13-yard run (Nickson pass failed)—7 plays, 90 yards, in 1:48.

2nd

UF: Baker 14-yard pass from Leak (Hetland kick)—6 plays, 49 yards, in 2:58.

3rd

UF: Leak 4-yard run (Hetland kick)—3 plays, 69 yards, in 1:00.

00:16 UF: Hetland 29-yard field goal—6 plays, 24 yards, in 2:10.

4th

VU: Smith 10-yard pass from Nickson (Nickson pass failed)—8 plays, 74 yards, in 3:43.

VU: Bennett 31-yard pass from Nickson (Hahnfeldt kick)—7 plays, 54 yards, in 1:32.

Team Statistics

	UF	VU
First Downs	18	19
Net Yards Rushing	88	93
Net Yards Passing	242	298
Passes (Comp-Att-Int)	19-28-3	27-44-1
Total Offense (Plays-Yards)	61-330	67-391
Fumbles-Lost	2-0	1-0
Penalties-Yards	6-53	3-33
Punts-Yards	6-253	7-206
Punt Returns-Yards	5-62	2-12
Kickoff Returns-Yards	3-66	5-77
Interceptions-Yards	1-1	3-4
Fumble Returns-Yards	0-0	0-0
Possession Time	31:55	28:05
Sacks By-Yards	3-18	4-24

Tony Joiner (19) breaks up the pass to Vanderbilt's George Smith in the end zone during the first quarter.
Doug Finger/The Gainesville Sun

Florida quarterback Chris Leak peers out from underneath Vanderbilt's Ray Brown after scoring the first touchdown of the game on a 4-yard run. *Tracy Wilcox/The Gainesville Sun*

"We just have to look at the mistakes and go back and fix them," Leak said. "There are a lot of good things to take from this game."

One positive is the fact the Gators threw the ball vertically, getting it into the hands of the wide receivers, who came up big.

Dallas Baker caught a 14-yard TD pass early in the second quarter and finished with seven receptions for 135 yards. Caldwell added eight receptions for 68 yards.

"I thought our execution today was pretty good if you take away the three picks," Meyer said. "But you can't take away the picks. It's something that he has to work on. But we made a concerted effort to throw the ball downfield today. We matched up well at wide receiver today.

"I thought our receivers played tremendous. They are our best players right now."

There were other positives as well:

• The Gators blocked two punts, one by cornerback Ryan Smith that set up UF's first touchdown, and one by free safety Reggie Nelson.

• Leak added a dimension to his goal-line game by running for two touchdowns, both from 4 yards out.

• Chris Hetland ended his slump with a 29-yard field goal in the third quarter.

• The defense played well early and then came up with enough plays to preserve the UF victory in the fourth quarter.

It was enough to add up to a victory that put the Gators in position to win the division a little later in the day.

On a brilliant fall day, it appeared the Gators were going to be able to experience a nice, relaxing end to this game after Hetland's 29-yard field goal in the closing seconds of the third quarter gave Florida a commanding 25-6 lead.

But nothing seems to come easy for this team, and that's the way it played out again in a nervous and frenetic fourth quarter that saw the Commodores threatening to pull off the upset.

Vandy climbed back into the game with a 10-yard pass from Chris Nickson to George Smith to make it a 25-12 game with 11:33 to play.

With the depth-shy UF defense growing weary, the Florida offense did nothing to help.

On UF's third offensive play following the Vandy score, Leak, attempting to throw deep to Baker, was intercepted for the third time, giving the Commodores the ball on their own 25.

Nickson hit Earl Bennett over the middle for 36 yards to put Vandy in scoring range. But the UF defense came up big, when tackle Ray McDonald nailed running back Cassen Jackson-Garrison one yard short of a first down on a fourth-and-2 play from the UF 11.

UF's offense, however, went three and out, giving the ball right back to Vanderbilt.

This time, the Commodores converted a fourth-down play with an 11-yard pass from Nickson to Bennett. Two plays later, Nickson and Bennett hooked up for a 31-yard TD pass. Suddenly, it was a 25-19 game with 2:30 still left in the game.

"I felt that our guys at the end of the game on defense got pushed in a little bit," Meyer said. "That is a product of fatigue and the schedule that we play."

Luckily for Florida, the defense did not have to play another play.

Vanderbilt's onside-kick attempt was recovered by Baker and the Gators were able to run out the clock and keep their championship run on track.

Then they became champions.

"We haven't been 8-1 around here in a long time," senior defensive tackle Steven Harris said. "It feels good. We're just trying to keep moving forward."

The Gators are moving forward—to Atlanta. ◥

Chad Richetson, 22, cheers the Gators during the first quarter of the LSU game in Gainesville. *Doug Finger/The Gainesville Sun*

Too Much Nonsense

By Pat Dooley, *Sun* sports writer

Hello, my name is nonsense. It used to be noise, as in "noise in the system." That was a different coach. Now it's nonsense, as in "the Florida nonsense."

It's Urban Meyer's catch phrase for me, you and the family across the street with the Gator flag still flying. It's the guy who just made reservations for Arizona in early January. It's the guy who called Florida athletic director Jeremy Foley when the Gators were voted No. 2 in the irrelevant Associated Press poll and talked how important that was for the national championship game.

It's the woman who believes Tim Tebow can win the Heisman...this year. It's anyone who still believes Chris Leak can win it. It's the fan with the Reggie Nelson desktop wallpaper and the Percy Harvin screensaver. It's the student who stopped Ray McDonald between classes to get a quick picture of himself and his new best friend.

It's questions from the media about the possibility of winning a national championship, about the swagger being back, about just how good this defense has been, about anything except Auburn.

"It's part of the deal you're going to get at Florida," tight end Tate Casey said. "There's going to be a lot of talking going on. But I think we've matured as players to handle it."

Nonsense does beat the alternative, which is noise, and not the good kind.

The difference is that nonsense comes with winning, while noise comes with losing.

Nonsense is powered by delirium. Every victory is another kerosene-soaked log on the fire. It makes people say the strangest things.

And it makes us in the media reach for new adjectives and heightened levels of hyperbole to describe a team that has made it halfway through the season, halfway through its SEC schedule and halfway through the four-game gauntlet without a loss.

"I worry about that," Meyer said. "Questions about the swagger and did we win The Swamp back? Every question I get fuels it. It will be a real intense meeting. The seniors will tell me if there is a problem. Our seniors will have to help us because you know the freshmen are out there reading that stuff."

Not from me, of course, because according to my e-mails I'm the most anti-Gator person to ever live. Still, I can pile on the nonsense with the best of them. Just ask my wife.

Meyer has seen plenty of the Florida nonsense in his short time on the job. He has pointed several times to questions he received last year about the possibility that his third-team tailback (DeShawn Wynn) might leave early for the NFL. He has talked about third uncles who think their guy should be starting, about Leak's statement at SEC Media Days that his goal is to throw 50 touchdown passes, about anything other than the next game.

It's hardly unique to Florida, but it is a bigger bubble of nonsense. More fans, more media than most places. Higher expectations than some because of the 1990s. It can create the worst daydream, the one where the Gators are in the Fiesta Bowl on January 8. If you're thinking about January, you're not ready to play in October.

To be 6-0 is great, but all it has really done is make the Gators bowl eligible.

"It makes you walk with your head held a little higher to be a Gator," said linebacker Brandon Siler of the 6-0 start. "I think this team is mature enough. We're an older team. I don't think anybody's going to go off being cocky or change their attitude. If they did, I'd be disappointed."

You hear this all the time. Players say they won't let the accolades get to them, that they won't read their press clippings. Ray McDonald said that he hardly ever reads the paper. Gee, thanks a lot.

But it's more than the media. It's the students and the fans at Burrito Bros., and the waitress at Gator City. You keep hearing how great you are and you lose focus on making sure you stay that great.

Meyer has a plan to keep these guys on the right track.

"We make practice very hard. We make meetings very hard," he said. "We have very interactive teaching. If a player doesn't know the answer to a question, he's not paying attention. I worry about when they leave here."

That's when the nonsense really begins.

But isn't it just part of being a college football player?

The nonsense isn't the problem. It's how you handle it that matters. ▲

Dallas Baker greets Gators fans in the stands after the game against Kentucky. *Tracy Wilcox/The Gainesville Sun*

Spurrier's Return a Losing One

By Robbie Andreu, *Sun* sports writer

A football coach with timeouts in his pocket has the power to stall fate, maybe even influence it a little bit.

Florida coach Urban Meyer had that power. He had the chance to delay the inevitable three times. But after using one timeout to put the freeze on fate—and South Carolina place-kicker Ryan Succop—Meyer was like everyone else holding their breath and wiping sweating palms with eight seconds remaining in The Swamp.

He needed to know. He couldn't wait any longer.

"We had two timeouts and I was going to burn one," Meyer said. "But I couldn't stand it."

So, he held onto his timeouts and sent his field-goal block team onto the field with one last thought in his mind: "We're going to block it."

And that is exactly what fate had in store for Meyer and the Florida Gators.

Jarvis Moss, a 6-foot-6 defensive end from Texas, leaped into the air and blocked Succop's 47-yard, game-deciding field goal attempt with his right palm to give the No. 6 Gators a heart-pounding 17-16 victory over South Carolina and former UF coaching legend Steve Spurrier on the last play of the game.

"That was a great ending," Meyer said.

The dramatic block sent a sold-out Swamp (90,703) into a frenzy and moved the Eastern Division champion Gators to 9-1 on the season. Somehow, Florida remains in the hunt for the national title.

So, is it fate that keeps propelling these unlikely Gators forward?

"This might be the year of the Gators," Spurrier said.

Moss, for one, is embracing the possibility.

"There is no question in my mind we're going to end up in Arizona (for the national title game on January 8)," Moss said.

For sure, all the orange and blue karma is good coming out of this victory.

Moss not only blocked the final kick, he blocked Succop's extra-point attempt earlier in the fourth quarter that kept the Gators within six, 16-10.

After Chris Leak led the Gators on a clutch 80-yard touchdown drive that culminated with a 12-yard TD run by No. 2 quarterback Tim Tebow, the Gators took their first lead of the game with Chris Hetland's PAT with only 3:03 to play.

The drive included a 6-yard run by Tebow on fourth-and-1 from UF's own 29.

"There was never any question. We were going for that," Meyer said.

Had the Gators punted there, they might not have seen the ball again against a USC offense that

The Gators congratulate quarterback Tim Tebow (15) after he scored the game-winning touchdown against South Carolina.
Rob C. Witzel/The Gainesville Sun

	1st	2nd	3rd	4th	Final
South Carolina	7	0	0	9	16
Florida	0	7	0	10	17

Scoring Summary

1st

SC: Davis 4-yard run (Succop kick)—13 plays, 80 yards, in 6:10.

2nd

UF: Baker 21-yard pass from Leak (Hetland kick)—7 plays, 78 yards, in 3:19.

4th

SC: Succop 47-yard field goal—11 plays, 51 yards, in 5:49.

UF: Hetland 22-yard field goal—10 plays, 75 yards, in 4:02.

SC: Davis 14-yard run (Succop kick blocked)—6 plays, 80 yards, in 2:36.

UF: Tebow 12-yard run (Hetland kick)—11 plays, 80 yards, in 5:10.

Team Statistics

	SC	UF
First Downs	23	28
Net Yards Rushing	135	147
Net Yards Passing	275	254
Passes (Comp-Att-Int)	24-34-0	19-29-1
Total Offense (Plays-Yards)	62-410	61-401
Fumbles-Lost	0-0	0-0
Penalties-Yards	10-85	4-49
Punts-Yards	2-79	2-72
Punt Returns-Yards	0-0	2-16
Kickoff Returns-Yards	3-50	2-26
Interceptions-Yards	1-3	0-0
Fumble Returns-Yards	0-0	0-0
Possession Time	30:31	29:29
Sacks By-Yards	2-10	0-0

Jarvis Moss (94) blocks the potential game-winning field goal as time expires during the Gators' 17-16 win over the Gamecocks.
Rob C. Witzel/The Gainesville Sun

Dallas Baker juggles a pass from Chris Leak, which he eventually reeled in for a 21-yard, second-quarter touchdown.
Doug Finger/The Gainesville Sun

had been going up and down the field and eating up the clock.

That same offense quickly moved the Gamecocks into position to win the game in the closing seconds. In fact, for a brief moment, it appeared Succop would only have to hit a chip-shot to win the game after quarterback Blake Mitchell completed a pass to wide receiver Sidney Rice inside the UF 15. But the play was wiped out by a motion penalty on Rice.

One play later, Succop came on to try to win the game for the Gamecocks.

Instead, Moss won it for the Gators after having to almost beg his way on to the field. Co-defensive coordinator Charlie Strong, who coaches the punt-block team, had planned to have defensive end Derrick Harvey in Moss' place, but relented and let Moss go in.

During the timeout before the kick, defensive tackles Ray McDonald and Steven Harris told Moss they were going to cave in the right side of USC's line and give him a chance to jump up and make the block.

"The first thing Jarvis Moss said in front of the team in the locker room was thanks to Steven Harris and Ray McDonald," Meyer said. "In the huddle before the kick they told him they were going to clear things out and they did."

Moss said he reached up and caught the ball flush with his right palm.

"That was the biggest play I've ever made in my career," he said. "I'm so happy to be a Gator and come through for my teammates. It started with Steven Harris and Ray McDonald being able to double-team a guy and knock him back. That gave me room to get up and use my jumping ability and block the kick."

Moss came through for his teammates and prevented Succop from doing the same for his.

"It is frustrating," Succop said. "Special teams had a chance to help out the team tonight, but we couldn't get it done. It is very disappointing."

Succop also had a 47-yard field goal attempt blocked by McDonald

midway through the third quarter that would have broken a 7-7 tie.

After Succop and Hetland traded field goals in the fourth quarter, the Gamecocks took the lead on a 14-yard TD run by tailback Mike Davis with 8:13 left in the game. Moss, however, kept it a six-point game (16-10) by blocking Succop's PAT with his left forearm.

The Gators then went on what turned out to be the game-winning drive.

Leak, who finished with 254 yards passing, including a 21-yard TD pass to Dallas Baker in the first half, kept the drive going with some crucial runs, the most critical being an 8-yard run on third-and-8 from the USC 20. On the next play, Tebow powered over the right side for a 12-yard run.

From that point on, the Gators found themselves hanging on.

Then, on the game's last play, fate smiled on the Gators.

"I think we've really got something special going on now," Moss said.

Youth is Served on Senior Day

By Robbie Andreu, *Sun* sports writer

On the same day they gave a Swamp farewell to 21 seniors, the Florida Gators gave us a glimpse of their future.

It looks pretty promising. And very skilled. And very fast.

With the senior starters giving way early to the true and redshirt freshmen, the No. 3 Gators, as expected, overwhelmed Division I-AA Western Carolina 62-0 before 90,233 at Florida Field.

The victory gives the Gators (10-1) their fifth 10-win regular season in history and makes them 13-0 at home over the past two seasons.

On Senior Day, the freshmen and redshirt freshmen turned out to be the story.

"Take a look at all the young people that have played this year and you can see Florida's future," UF coach Urban Meyer said.

Florida's highly rated 2006 recruiting class is looking better and better all the time.

"Every time a freshman made a play, we'd say, '06, '06, '06," true freshman tailback/kick returner Brandon James said. "I think we have lot of good things to go (in the future)."

James drew the '06 chant from his fellow true freshmen. He returned a punt 77 yards for a touchdown and broke the school record for punt return yards in a game with 155.

James was just one of many freshman playmakers on a day when the Gators outgained WCU 582 yards to 59.

Here's a sampling:

• Running the entire offense for the first time in his young career, Tim Tebow completed 10 of 12 passes for 200 yards and two touchdowns and rushed for an additional 47 yards and two scores.

• Wide receiver Jarred Fayson lined up at quarterback in the shotgun and ran for 77 yards and a touchdown.

• Wide receiver Riley Cooper caught three passes—all for touchdowns—for 82 yards.

• Tailback Mon Williams led the Gators in rushing with 95 yards, all coming in the fourth quarter.

• Linebackers Brandon Spikes and Dustin Doe, starting for the first time, combined for 10 tackles.

Freshmen, freshmen everywhere, making plays and painting a bright future for UF.

"I think the experience was great," said Fayson, who was a quarterback at Tampa Hillsborough. "A lot of freshmen got to come out and play. We had a lot of opportunities and we made the most of them."

Tebow certainly did. He was nearly flawless running the whole offensive package, as opposed to his usually limited "Tebow package." UF fans have been clamoring

Mon Williams carries the ball upfield in the final quarter during the blowout of Western Carolina University.
Doug Finger/The Gainesville Sun

	1st	2nd	3rd	4th	Final
Western Carolina	0	0	0	0	0
Florida	14	20	14	14	62

Scoring Summary

1st

UF: Wynn 26-yard run (Hetland kick)—7 plays, 65 yards, in 2:19.

UF: Wynn 7-yard run (Nappy kick)—7 plays, 29 yards, in 4:40.

2nd

UF: Cooper 7-yard pass from Leak (Nappy kick blocked)—6 plays, 73 yards, in 2:43.

UF: Tebow 20-yard run (Nappy kick)—5 plays, 58 yards, in 2:57.

UF: James 77-yard punt return (Phillips kick).

3rd

UF: Tebow 1-yard run (Phillips kick)—8 plays, 63 yards, in 3:50.

UF: Fayson 8-yard run (Phillips kick)—6 plays, 56 yards, in 3:08.

4th

UF: Cooper 55-yard pass from Tebow (Phillips kick)—5 plays, 80 yards, in 1:06.

UF: Cooper 20-yard pass from Tebow (Phillips kick)—7 plays, 68 yards, in 4:21.

Team Statistics

	WCU	UF
First Downs	4	27
Net Yards Rushing	24	282
Net Yards Passing	35	300
Passes (Comp-Att-Int)	5-12-0	19-24-0
Total Offense (Plays-Yards)	40-59	58-582
Fumbles-Lost	1-0	0-0
Penalties-Yards	6-35	11-90
Punts-Yards	10-423	0-0
Punt Returns-Yards	0-0	8-171
Kickoff Returns-Yards	8-148	1-12
Interceptions-Yards	0-0	0-0
Fumble Returns-Yards	0-0	0-0
Possession Time	30:08	29:52
Sacks By-Yards	0-0	1-6

Running back DeShawn Wynn falls into the end zone for one of his two first-quarter touchdowns. The play was reviewed, but the ruling stood.

Doug Finger/The Gainesville Sun

Offensive lineman Phil Trautwein loses his helmet as Jarred Fayson (11) scrambles for extra yardage.
Tracy Wilcox/The Gainesville Sun

for Tebow to get a chance to throw the ball and he did against Western Carolina.

"He earned that right. He's been practicing very well," Meyer said. "He's there. He can run the offense. He's a full-functioning quarterback at the University of Florida."

Tebow threw touchdown passes of 20 and 55 yards to Cooper, one of UF's fastest young receivers who has seen most of his time on special teams. Cooper also caught a 7-yard touchdown pass from senior quarterback Chris Leak in the first half.

"A lot of freshmen stepped up today," Cooper said. "That's a good sign for the future.

"Everyone keeps asking me (what it's like to score a touchdown in The Swamp), but I can't explain it. It's an incredible feeling with everyone cheering for you."

Another freshman creating quite a buzz in The Swamp was Williams, the true freshman tailback from Mesquite, Texas. He is one of the fastest members of the '06 recruiting class and it appears he's starting to pick up the offense and learning how to practice, Meyer said.

"He's another guy, he's not been consistent," Meyer said. "I was glad to see that. The last week and a half of practice he's shown up.

"He went through a month and a half where some third uncles were involved with opinions (on why Williams should be playing) and everything else as opposed to go out and practice real hard."

While the freshmen wrote much of the game's story, it was still Senior Day—and the seniors quickly put this game in shape early to hand over to the freshmen (and eventually walk-ons).

Senior tailback DeShawn Wynn had touchdown runs of 26 and 7 yards in the first quarter, then Leak put the game comfortably in hand with the TD pass to Cooper to make it a 20-0 game early in the second quarter.

Wynn carried the ball only four times for 32 yards, while Leak completed nine of 12 passes for 100 yards and a touchdown.

"All the seniors were on the sideline rooting the freshmen on," Leak said. "It was fun to get a win like that in my last game in The Swamp."

"My emotions were everywhere (coming out of the tunnel for the last time). I just tried to enjoy it and take it all in. I'm real happy about it." ▸

A group of fans hold signs and chant for senior Tim Higgins during the game against Western Carolina. The fans got their wish when Urban Meyer put Higgins in for some plays in the second half. *Tracy Wilcox/The Gainesville Sun*

Higgins is Florida's 'Rudy'

By Pat Dooley, *Sun* sports writer

It wasn't quite *Rudy*, but it was close. There probably won't be any movie rights, but it was no less inspirational. Tim Higgins sat in the meeting room where he spent so many hours knowing he wasn't going to play answering questions Saturday about playing. On Senior Day, nobody expected to be talking to this senior.

"I don't deserve a chance to be a Florida Gator," he said. "I don't deserve to get on the field to play. I definitely don't deserve to get the ball in my hands.

"This is a dream come true."

Urban Meyer would disagree that Higgins, a receiver from Northfield, Michigan, didn't deserve what he received on a beautiful Saturday afternoon in The Swamp. He has seen the 5-foot-7, 162-pounder take hit after hit, doing whatever was necessary without the carrot dangling at the end of a stick.

Meyer put Higgins on scholarship this year because he was so impressed with the effort, the drive, the desire to help others get better.

"I saw a little guy who did everything we asked him to do," Meyer said. "If you said, 'Tim, get over here and run into two guys and get your helmet knocked off,' he'd do it and do it again.

"He's a classy guy who is going to graduate. Watch what Tim Higgins is going to do the next 20 years."

Unlike Rudy Ruettiger at Notre Dame, Higgins had no trouble getting into school at Florida. He was a National Merit Scholar. He chose Florida because his father, Kevin, now the head coach at The Citadel, had a friend on the UF staff when Higgins was young and he grew up a Gator fan.

But like Rudy, he had some help getting on the field. A letter appeared on Meyer's desk earlier this week asking him to play Higgins. Members of the Fellowship of Christian Athletes made signs—"We (heart) Higgins"—and passed out pamphlets encouraging Meyer to put Higgins in the game. They chanted his name late in Florida's blowout win.

"People were screaming, 'Give me Higgins!'" Meyer said. "So I gave them Higgins."

When No. 37 ran onto the field, it was deja vu for anyone who has seen *Rudy* multiple times. Same strange sight of a little guy among the giants, same loud cheer from those who had been yelling for him, even the same choppy steps and the reach for his chinstrap to buckle it up.

He should have the mannerisms down. He watched the movie this week "three or four times."

The story gets better. Higgins is a wide receiver, but Meyer wanted to be sure he got the ball so he told him to get with quarterback Tim Tebow because Higgins would be going in at running back.

Tebow, the quarterback who outweighs his new tailback by almost 60 pounds, showed Higgins the steps required to run the play that would be called.

"He had to line me up because I didn't know where I was going," Higgins said. "I've never taken a handoff at any level."

If they ever make a movie, the actor playing Higgins will probably break tackles on his way to a big gain, maybe even a touchdown. Higgins was stopped for no gain.

Didn't matter.

"All the shots I've taken on scout team, all of the times catching a ball over the middle and getting blown up, all the sweating and bleeding, wondering if it would ever pay off," he said. "There were times when I was frustrated, but I was lucky enough to be brought up in a family where you don't quit.

"I always believed God had a plan for me, but sometimes I wondered why I was here."

He's here to get an education, a history major who plans to teach and coach. And he was here for Saturday.

Until that one carry, Higgins was best known to teammates for being in the National Spelling Bee twice where his best finish was a tie for 22nd. But that didn't compare with what happened on Senior Day.

"I thought coming out of the tunnel was exhilarating," he said. "What a rush to have this be the culmination of everything."

Tim Higgins will never forget his last game in The Swamp. But it's not the end. It's just the beginning. ▲

In the game at running back, Tim Higgins is tackled by Western Carolina defenders at the line of scrimmage. *Doug Finger/The Gainesville Sun*

Gators Hold Back 'Noles for 11th Win

By Pat Dooley, *Sun* sports writer

For Florida fans, the game had a familiar feel. Unfortunately for Florida State fans, it did as well.

The Gators kept another team in the game with missed field goals and mistakes, but again found a way to win in the end, 21-14 over the Seminoles.

"It's called winning and losing," Florida coach Urban Meyer said.

It was the sixth straight win for Meyer over Florida's three biggest rivals (FSU, Georgia and Tennessee)—the only time in history that has happened—and gave the Gators a three-game winning streak over the Seminoles and their second straight win at Bobby Bowden Field.

For senior quarterback Chris Leak, it was another satisfying win in a big game.

"It's a great feeling," Leak said, "to beat a legendary coach like Bobby Bowden twice here at their place."

It was Leak who came through in the fourth quarter after Florida had allowed FSU to rally from a 14-0 deficit to tie the score. Leak engineered a 74-yard scoring drive completing 7-of-8 passes including what turned out to be the game-winning score on a 25-yard pass to fellow senior Dallas Baker in the back of the end zone.

"It's a credit to our seniors," Leak said. "It was just about making plays when they had to be made."

Leak's pass to Baker came on a third-and-9 play and gave Florida the lead with 10:22 to play. The Gators then turned to their defense, which stopped FSU on three fourth-down plays on the next three drives.

"It's frustrating that we haven't been able to put a complete game together," said cornerback Ryan Smith, who had one of UF's three interceptions in the third quarter. "But it's like I was telling some of the guys—as long as we keep winning, it works."

The victory may not have helped Florida's slim hopes for a berth in the BCS national title game, but it certainly keeps them alive and may have secured UF a berth in a BCS bowl game. Florida plays Arkansas in Atlanta next Saturday for the SEC championship.

Asked about style points and the BCS standings, Meyer said, "Here's our style: at Tennessee, a Kentucky team that's 7-4 (now 7-5), Alabama, LSU, Auburn at their place, Georgia and this game. So much for style. If that's what's making the decision, I stand by what I said last week. It's over. Implode it (the BCS system)."

Florida looked as if it was going to pile up plenty of style points, gaining 266 yards in the first half and taking a 14-0 lead despite two more missed field goals by Chris Hetland.

Florida State tight end Brandon Warren (1) fails to catch a potential game-tying touchdown in the second half.
Rob C. Witzel/The Gainesville Sun

	1st	2nd	3rd	4th	Final
Florida	**7**	**7**	**0**	**7**	**21**
Florida State	**0**	**0**	**7**	**7**	**14**

Scoring Summary

1st
UF: Caldwell 66-yard pass from Leak (Hetland kick)—5 plays, 78 yards, in 2:09.

2nd
UF: Harvin 41-yard run (Hetland kick)—3 plays, 68 yards, in 1:02.

3rd
FS: Surratt 1-yard run (Cismesia kick)—4 plays, 44 yards, in 0:39.

4th
FS: Carr 25-yard pass from Weatherford (Cismesia kick)—4 plays, 41 yards, in 1:17.

UF: Baker 25-yard pass from Leak (Hetland kick)—10 plays, 74 yards, in 3:55.

Team Statistics

	UF	FS
First Downs	16	11
Net Yards Rushing	105	46
Net Yards Passing	283	189
Passes (Comp-Att-Int)	21-35-0	18-43-3
Total Offense (Plays-Yards)	67-388	61-235
Fumbles-Lost	1-1	2-0
Penalties-Yards	7-65	4-27
Punts-Yards	8-332	5-220
Punt Returns-Yards	1-8	2-12
Kickoff Returns-Yards	3-47	3-94
Interceptions-Yards	3-1	0-0
Fumble Returns-Yards	0-0	0-0
Possession Time	33:43	26:17
Sacks By-Yards	2-20	1-1

Wide receiver Dallas Baker picks up a key first down on Florida's eventual game-winning drive against the Florida State Seminoles.
Rob C. Witzel/The Gainesville Sun

Florida receiver Percy Harvin is consoled on a stretcher by his teammates and FSU receiver Damon McDaniel, a high school classmate, after Harvin was injured during the first half. *Rob C. Witzel/The Gainesville Sun*

Leak hit Andre Caldwell on a bubble screen while FSU was blitzing, and Caldwell took it 66 yards for a score. A 41-yard touchdown run by Percy Harvin made it 14-0.

But in the third quarter, FSU rallied despite three interceptions from FSU quarterback Drew Weatherford. With Harvin having to leave the field on a motorized cart after suffering a neck injury and tailback DeShawn Wynn out with a shoulder injury, the offense stalled, managing only 32 yards in the third quarter.

FSU scored late in the third quarter and again early in the fourth quarter to tie the game before Leak drove the Gators to the winning score.

"We had a bad third quarter," Meyer said. "There was no life on the sidelines, no juice. When the coaches have to get the team up, you have a problem. We were in a funk, I can't explain it."

But Florida responded with the touchdown drive that won the game and left FSU with another difficult loss.

"It was a very disappointing year," Bowden said. "I think we'd get a very unanimous vote on that."

Despite Florida's close win, the Gators left Bowden impressed.

"I think they're doggone good," he said. "They look darn second to that 1996 team they had. That's how they looked to me."

Florida finished the game with a decided edge on offense—388 yards to 235 for FSU—as Leak passed for 283 yards. Other than Harvin's touchdown run, the Gators managed only 64 yards rushing on 31 carries.

"That's the most disappointing thing," Meyer said, "that our line got handled by their defensive line."

Still, the Gators escaped with yet another win. In its last four big games—Georgia, Vanderbilt, South Carolina and FSU—Florida won by a total of 21 points.

"Playing teams like we've been playing," said reserve quarterback Tim Tebow, "it's hard to run up the score." ◣

Adam Jenkins, 33, and his brother Paul, 24, cheer on the Gators as they face the Arkansas Razorbacks for the SEC championship. *Doug Finger/The Gainesville Sun*

11-1

By Pat Dooley, *Sun* sports writer

I know they're driving you crazy. I know there are times when you can't believe what you're seeing, especially when Chris Hetland runs out onto the field to try another field goal. I know their coach is aging in front of our eyes.

"You see these gray hairs right here," Urban Meyer said. "Next year about October I'll be bald."

I know it seems like you see the same game every week. I know that Florida didn't do itself any BCS favors with another close game that allows the talking heads to pick away at the warts.

But I also know this—Florida is 11-1. Is there anybody out there who wouldn't have poured the good stuff into a glass and toasted 11-1 at the beginning of the season?

Does it matter that they continue to let teams hang around in games that look like they were heading for easy victories? Does it matter that they are still committing crucial penalties and missing field goals and inexplicably dropping handoffs and making you want to scream?

Not really.

Not now.

All that really matters is the Gators are 11-1 heading to Atlanta.

Do you think the way they won again during this Groundhog Day of a season mattered to the fans who were chanting Meyer's name as he left the field or screaming "Orange...Blue" as they exited Doak Campbell Stadium?

In this place where so many coaches have struggled so mightily, Florida has won two straight.

That's why I didn't even have to finish the question to Chris Leak in the cramped interview area under the stadium where so many Gator teams have had to listen to Seminole chops and taunts.

"Chris, can you talk about how it feels..."

"To be 2-0 at this place?" Leak asked, finishing the question.

To be 2-0 on the field named after the winningest coach in college football history?

To have completed 7-of-8 passes on the game-winning touchdown drive including a 25-yarder to your buddy Dallas Baker for the touchdown?

"It's a great way to finish off my career against them," Leak said with a toothy grin.

We all know that FSU is not the FSU that tormented Steve Spurrier at times during his career as Florida's coach or even the FSU that beat Ron Zook twice in three tries. But it's still FSU, another rival that wakes up today wondering how it lost to this Florida team.

"Nobody else has three rivals like we do," Meyer said. "That's what makes this job the best in America."

It certainly makes it one of the most stressful, especially when you keep following the same plan to win, and I don't mean the one Meyer draws up each week. That one doesn't include two missed field goals, your best playmaker being carted off the field or your one reliable tailback leaving with a shoulder injury.

It doesn't include a fumble on a reverse when nobody touches the ball carrier. And I guarantee it doesn't include the opponent getting back into the game by throwing three interceptions in a quarter, which is exactly what FSU did.

You should never have to apologize for winning 11 games in a season that still has two to go.

"To the guys in that locker room and the guys that matter, it's 11-1 and six straight against our rivals," Meyer said. "I think people understand that was a tough game."

Are they perfect? Not even close. Are they frustrating at times? No question. But do they have a knack for winning football games? Absolutely.

Some way, somehow, they are one controversial call away from possibly being perfect. If that's not enough to impress voters or computer geeks, so be it. It's the flawed system that we live with every fall that makes Florida have to beg for acceptance and answer questions about style points.

After the SEC championship game in Atlanta, Florida will have played 10 teams who are bowl eligible. Meyer is now 20-4 in two years as the Gator coach. Florida is 11-1.

Get it straight—that's what matters. ▲

University of Florida fan and Gainesville resident Ben Keator, 24, cheers on his Florida Gators while making his way to Doak Campbell Stadium in Tallahassee. *Tracy Wilcox/The Gainesville Sun*

12 Wins, 1 SEC Title

By Robbie Andreu, *Sun* sports writer

The six-year drought is over. The Florida Gators are champions again, rulers of their world in the SEC for first time since 2000.

Now, will the 12-1 Gators have a chance to play for another championship, an even bigger one?

That will be decided today when the final BCS standings come out.

There is a chance that the Gators could be Arizona bound to play No. 1 Ohio State for the national title on January 8.

After Southern Cal, the No. 2 BCS team, fell to UCLA earlier in the day, Florida did what it needed to do in the Georgia Dome, overcoming a disastrous start to the second half to rally for a dramatic 38-28 victory over Arkansas.

"It's indescribable," said senior Florida quarterback Chris Leak, who ran for a touchdown and threw for one. "I can't describe the emotions I'm feeling right now. My emotions are everywhere."

It was that kind of night, that kind of victory, for the Gators.

"It feels good to finally get an SEC championship," said senior wide receiver Jemalle Cornelius, who had a key 17-yard run on a fake punt that helped shift momentum late in the third quarter. "This is why you come to the University of Florida.

"We had a rough couple of years, but Coach (Urban) Meyer and his staff came in here and picked us up and showed us how to win. I'm feeling real good right now."

The Gators might be feeling even better today if the Gators gain enough support to pass Michigan to the No. 2 spot in the BCS.

"We're going to enjoy this win and think about that tomorrow morning," Cornelius said. "We definitely want a chance to go out and play. We played a tough schedule and we found ways to win games. We feel we deserve a chance to play in the Big Show."

Said Leak: "Knowing how hard these guys have worked, we know if we get an opportunity (to play

for the national title) it will be deserved. We fought through a lot of adversity this season. It would be a great deal for us to play for a title."

Winning the SEC title was huge enough.

After blowing a 17-7 lead early in the third quarter, the Gators won the game in the fourth quarter. Game MVP Percy Harvin, a speedy true freshman wide receiver, sprinted 67 yards for a touchdown to give UF a 31-21 lead with 14:22 remaining.

Arkansas responded with 29-yard touchdown pass on a trick play to cut the lead back to three.

The Gators regained control of the game by driving 80 yards in eight plays, culminating with a 5-yard TD pass from wide receiver Andre Caldwell to tight end Tate

From the sideline, Jarvis Moss celebrates a second-quarter touchdown by Percy Harvin against the Razorbacks.
Doug Finger/The Gainesville Sun

	1st	2nd	3rd	4th	Final
Arkansas	0	7	14	7	28
Florida	3	14	7	14	38

Scoring Summary

1st
UF: Hetland 33-yard field goal—6 plays, 47 yards, in 2:25.

2nd
UF: Leak 9-yard run (Hetland kick)—1 play, 9 yards, in 0:29.

UF: Harvin 37-yard pass from Leak (Hetland kick)—8 plays, 74 yards, in 3:23.

AR: Monk 48-yard pass from Dick (Davis kick)—3 plays, 66 yards, in 2:07.

3rd
AR: Jones 2-yard pass from McFadden (Davis kick)—7 plays, 32 yards, in 2:18.

AR: Robinson 40-yard interception return (Davis kick).

UF: Pierre-Louis 0-yard fumble recovery (Hetland kick).

4th
UF: Harvin 67-yard run (Hetland kick)—1 play, 67 yards, in 0:30.

AR: Jones 29-yard pass from Washington (Davis kick)—4 plays, 63 yards, in 1:53.

UF: Casey 5-yard pass from Caldwell (Hetland kick)—8 plays, 80 yards, in 3:25.

Team Statistics

	AR	UF
First Downs	18	17
Net Yards Rushing	132	202
Net Yards Passing	179	194
Passes (Comp-Att-Int)	12-26-3	17-31-2
Total Offense (Plays-Yards)	61-311	61-396
Fumbles-Lost	1-1	3-0
Penalties-Yards	5-25	8-67
Punts-Yards	6-176	6-224
Punt Returns-Yards	2-minus-4	5-29
Kickoff Returns-Yards	4-68	3-23
Interceptions-Yards	2-40	3-0
Fumble Returns-Yards	0-0	0-0
Possession Time	31:58	28:02
Sacks By-Yards	2-15	0-0

Percy Harvin races for a touchdown during the fourth quarter. Harvin was named Most Valuable Player of the game. *Rob C. Witzel/The Gainesville Sun*

Quarterback Chris Leak is at the bottom of the pile, but with enough yardage for a first down in the second quarter.
Tracy Wilcox/The Gainesville Sun

"[The senior class] earned the admiration of this coaching staff and the Gator Nation."

—Florida coach Urban Meyer

Casey to give UF a 38-28 cushion with 9:04 to play.

The defense, which stifled Arkansas tailback Darren McFadden all night, made the lead hold up with interceptions by free safety Reggie Nelson and cornerback Ryan Smith.

"I'd like to thank our senior class," Meyer said. "At some point, I'm not sure when, maybe 20 years from now, we're going to write a book and let everyone know what this senior class went through. They earned the admiration of this coaching staff and the Gator Nation."

The Gators, who haven't played a complete game all season (unless you count far inferior Western Carolina) appeared headed in that direction in the first half.

Chris Hetland even made a field goal attempt—a sure sign that things are going right.

Hetland was true from 34 yards out with 6:10 to play in the first quarter to give the Gators the early lead.

The Florida defense manhandled McFadden and the powerful Arkansas ground game in the first half, repeatedly giving the ball back to the UF offense.

The offense didn't take advantage of it, but the Florida special teams did.

With less than six minutes gone in the second quarter, true freshman wide receiver Jarred Fayson came clean on a punt attempt and blocked Jacob Skinner's kick, giving the Gators the ball on the Arkansas nine-yard line.

On the next play, Leak broke to the outside on a quarterback draw and scored to give UF a 10-0 lead.

After the defense earned another three-and-out against the Razorbacks' offense, the Florida offense finally came to life.

Leak found speedy wide receiver Percy Harvin behind the Hog secondary for a 37-yard touchdown pass to give the Gators a commanding 17-0 lead with only 4:02 remaining in the half.

At this point, it appeared the Gators might turn this game into their best of the season—and a rout of the Western Division champions.

It wasn't meant to be.

The Hogs stole some precious momentum back with 1:55 before halftime when cornerback Reggie Lewis fell down trying to cover Marcus Monk deep and Monk brought in the pass for a 48-yard scoring play.

That late momentum snowballed for Arkansas—and against

Florida—in the opening minutes of the second half, when the Razorbacks turned the 17-7 deficit into a 21-17 lead with less than seven minutes gone in the third quarter.

Leak threw an interception on the first play of the half that led to a quick touchdown—a 2-yard pass from McFadden to Felix Jones.

A few minutes later, Leak's shovel pass was intercepted by Arkansas defensive tackle Antwain Robinson and returned 40 yards for a touchdown.

Just like that, it was Arkansas 21, Florida 17.

But a few minutes later, the Hogs fumbled away their considerable momentum when Randy Kelly muffed an Eric Wilbur punt inside the 5-yard line and the ball was recovered in the end zone for a touchdown by freshman cornerback Wondy Pierre-Louis.

Just like that, the Gators had a 24-21 lead to carry into the fourth quarter.

Harvin made the lead grow to 31-21 with his 67-yard TD burst in the opening minute of the quarter. ▲

The Florida Gators celebrate with the
SEC Championship trophy following
their 38-28 win over Arkansas.
Rob C. Witzel/The Gainesville Sun

Gators Make Most of Chances

By Robbie Andreu, *Sun* sports writer

The last time the Florida Gators ventured into the desert in search of the national title, they were swept away by a sandstorm tinged in Nebraska red.

This time, the Gators were the ones who created the perfect storm, coming up with their best performance of this special season to shock No. 1 Ohio State 41-14 in the BCS Championship Game before a national television audience and 74,628 at the University of Phoenix Stadium.

Florida now holds the national championships in both football and basketball, the first school to ever achieve that remarkable feat in the same calendar year.

"I'm not surprised at all," senior wide receiver Dallas Baker said. "We had something to prove. Some people were predicting Ohio State to win 41-14. Well, it was 41-14 for the University of Florida.

"Nobody gave us a chance. Now, we can finally throw up a No. 1. We had a lot of doubters out there,

the media, the Ohio State fans. No one can doubt us now. We're national champs."

The No. 2 Gators (13-1) earned the title by making the most of every scoring opportunity on offense and by overwhelming Ohio State and Heisman Trophy-winning quarterback Troy Smith with superior speed on defense.

It was not supposed to happen this way. The Gators entered the game a 7-point underdog and many in the national media were talking about this Ohio State team possibly being one of the best in the history of college football.

"Our pregame speech was easy," said UF coach Urban Meyer, wearing a national championship jacket. "I don't want to say there was a lack of respect, but that's exactly what it was. For 30 days, our team got motivated and that's why they played so hard.

"I want to thank our seniors. We have 21 seniors who played as hard as they can. The senior class

is the reason we're here today. These seniors have earned my admiration. I love them. I can't tell you how much they mean to me. I told (senior quarterback) Chris Leak and (senior wide receiver) Jemalle Cornelius that we have no choice but to hang out together for the next 30 years because we're national champions."

The swarming Florida defense stymied Smith, sacking him five times and knocking him off his game. He completed only four of 14 passes for 35 yards and was intercepted once. The powerful Buckeyes managed only eight first downs and 82 yards of total offense.

"When you play defense like that, you don't lose," Meyer said. "Our defense did that all year against great teams."

In spite of losing his helmet to a hard block in the backfield, Earl Everett pursues and sacks Ohio State quarterback and Heisman winner Troy Smith.
Rob C. Witzel/The Gainesville Sun

	1st	2nd	3rd	4th	Final
Florida	14	20	0	7	41
Ohio State	7	7	0	0	14

Scoring Summary

1st

OSU: Ginn Jr. 93-yard kickoff return (Pettrey kick)

UF: Baker 14-yard pass from Leak (Hetland kick)—7 plays, 46 yards, in 4:13.

UF: Harvin 4-yard run (Hetland kick)—5 plays, 34 yards, in 2:37.

2nd

UF: Wynn 2-yard run from Taylor (Hetland kick)—10 plays, 71 yards, in 2:53.

OSU: Pittman 18-yard run (Pettrey kick)—4 plays, 64 yards, in 1:24.

UF: Hetland 42-yard field goal—9 plays, 32 yards, in 3:04.

UF: Hetland 40-yard field goal—4 plays, 6 yards, in 1:44.

UF: Caldwell 1-yard pass from Tebow (Hetland kick)—3 plays, 5 yards, in 1:05.

4th

UF: Tebow 1-yard run (Hetland kick)—8 plays, 39 yards, in 3:42.

Team Statistics

	UF	OSU
First Downs	21	8
Net Yards Rushing	156	47
Net Yards Passing	214	35
Passes (Comp-Att-Int)	26-37-0	4-14-1
Total Offense (Plays-Yards)	80-370	37-82
Fumbles-Lost	0-0	1-1
Penalties-Yards	6-50	5-50
Punts-Yards	4-177	6-227
Punt Returns-Yards	4-28	1-13
Kickoff Returns-Yards	1-33	6-193
Interceptions-Yards	1-0	0-0
Fumble Returns-Yards	1-9	0-0
Possession Time	40:08	19:12
Sacks By-Yards	5-51	1-7

Evading the OSU defense, tight end Cornelius Ingram makes a 20-yard gain during the first quarter.
Brian W. Kratzer/The Gainesville Sun

Chris Leak (12) and the Gators celebrate with Tim Tebow (15) after his 1-yard second-quarter touchdown pass to Andre Caldwell. *Tracy Wilcox/The Gainesville Sun*

Sophomore defensive end Derrick Harvey sacked Smith twice, recovered a fumble and was named the game's MVP.

"They're well coached. I can't say enough about those guys," Smith said of Florida. "They came out and fought for 60 minutes and did exactly what they needed to do to get the win. We came out and fought. If this is the worst thing that happens to us in life, I'm pretty cool with that."

Smith rarely had time to throw. When he did, UF's secondary usually had his receivers covered.

"When you pressure someone, you get them out of their rhythm," Harvey said. "He was rattled, running for his life. That's what a good defense made him do."

While Smith could get nothing going, UF's two-quarterback system of senior Chris Leak and true freshman Tim Tebow was close to flawless. Leak completed 25 of 36 passes for 213 yards and had no interceptions, while Tebow threw a touchdown and ran for a score.

His 1-yard run on fourth-and-goal came with 10:20 to play and put the game away.

In his final two games at UF, Leak won an SEC title and a national championship.

"We knew they were going to play zone coverage and Chris managed the game very well," Meyer said. "Winning championships is the way you're judged at Florida. It started back with Shane Matthews (in 1991). Chris is now one of the top two quarterbacks in Florida history (along with Danny Wuerffel). Only two have won a national championship in 100 years and Chris Leak is one of them."

The Buckeyes were stunned in defeat.

"We have to congratulate the University of Florida," Ohio State coach Jim Tressel said. "They did a great job in earning the national championship. No question about it.

"We scored on the first play of the game and from that point on we could not keep the pressure where we needed it to be."

Florida's night in the glare of the national spotlight could not have gotten off to a worse start.

Speedy All-America wide receiver Ted Ginn Jr. took the opening kickoff, found a gaping hole in the middle of the UF return team and sprinted untouched 93 yards for a touchdown and a 7-0 lead.

Ginn injured his ankle a little later in the quarter and did not return.

"When Ted Ginn went out, we covered their receivers and put a lot of pressure on the quarterback with the speed off the edge with Jarvis Moss and Derrick Harvey," Meyer said.

As shocking as Ginn's long TD run was, it didn't seem to faze the Gators, who had talked confidently all week that they felt they matched up well with the nation's No. 1 team.

Apparently, they were right.

The Gators responded to the early touchdown with one of their own and then dominated the rest of the half to build their 20-point lead.

The response to Ginn's long run was a 14-yard TD pass from Leak to wide receiver Dallas Baker to make it a 7-7 game with less than five minutes gone in the first quarter.

On OSU's next possession, the Florida defense forced a three-and-out. Following a short punt and a 15-yard personal foul penalty against the Buckeyes on the return, the Gators were back in scoring position again, at the OSU 34.

Four plays later, wide receiver Percy Harvin scored on a 4-yard run to give the Gators a 14-7 lead with 5:51 left in the first quarter.

While the offense was making the most of scoring opportunities, the speedy UF defense was shutting down the Heisman winner.

Cornerback Reggie Lewis intercepted a Smith pass on the UF 29 and then the Gators went on another scoring drive that culminated with a 2-yard TD run by Ohio native DeShawn Wynn on the first play of the second quarter.

Ohio State matched that score only three offensive plays later when junior tailback found open space off of left tackle and ran 18 yards for a touchdown to draw the Buckeyes within a touchdown, 21-14.

The rest of the first half belonged to the Gators. In a big way.

Chris Hetland was true on a season-long 42-yard field goal to give the Gators a 10-point lead with 6:00 remaining in the half.

Hetland upped it to 27-14 minutes later with a 40-yard field goal. It was the first game this season he made two field goals.

In the final minutes of the half, it was the Florida defense, appropriately enough, that set up the offense for an easy score that nearly put the game out of reach.

Defensive end Jarvis Moss sacked Smith from behind, Smith fumbled and Harvey recovered on the OSU 5.

On third-and-goal from the 1, Tebow threw a TD pass to Andre Caldwell to put the Gators ahead 34-14 with only 23 seconds left in the half.

The UF defense continued its domination in the second half and the Gators closed the deal with Tebow's touchdown run with 10:20 to play.

"We had too much speed and too many playmakers," Caldwell said. "We made a statement to the world that we're better than Ohio State."

1.8.2007 | OHIO STATE | W, 41-14

Florida Saves Best for Last

By Pat Dooley, *Sun* sports writer

How does it feel to wake up in Titletown today?

Just another national championship. Just another dominating performance in the biggest game of the year.

Not that it's getting boring.

Ask Chris Leak, whose vindication came in the form of that crystal trophy he held as if it was his first-born, a symbol of four years of everything.

"It's what I expected when I came here, to win a national championship," Leak said. "I can't put into words what it means."

Ask Cornelius Igram, who almost quit the team a year ago and instead became a major contributor in the national championship game with four catches for 58 yards.

"It's not hard to believe, it's hard to believe I almost left," Ingram said with a big smile. "It's the greatest feeling ever. I said winning the SEC was the greatest, this tops it."

Ask all of these guys who heard it all year, who heard it for a month.

Think they belong now, Michigan?

"There's a team that doesn't belong in this game," Deshawn Wynn said. "And it's not the Gators."

One thing you can say for the Gators, they know how to win a national championship.

They took a team that was supposed to be unbeatable and beat it down like it was UCF. They pushed so hard they caused the usually conservative Jim Tressel to go for it on fourth down from his own 29.

"Obviously, it was the wrong call," Tressel said.

This was the best we've seen this Florida team play this year. Who is the big-game coach now?

In their minds they were disrespected by the national media. They saw in one newspaper where a 42-14 score was predicted in favor of the other team.

Then they went out and came a point short of reversing it.

"Motivation was easy for the last 30 days," Urban Meyer said.

And so they were able to pass the crystal around, just as their basketball brethren did nine months ago. And they did so with a performance that will at least allow the 2006 Gators to enter the argument for best team in Gator history. Certainly, this was a game that is in the argument for best all-around performance ever.

And Leak gets into that best quarterback argument.

"He is officially one of the top two quarterbacks to play at the University of Florida," Meyer said.

It was a game that showed what we have seen all season—this is a

Dallas Baker scores the first touchdown of the game for the Gators on a 14-yard pass from Chris Leak.
Tracy Wilcox/The Gainesville Sun

120

Andre Caldwell sneaks into the end zone for a 1-yard touchdown on a pass from Tim Tebow. *Rob C. Witzel/The Gainesville Sun*

A happy Gator makes a confetti angel on the field during the postgame celebration of Florida's national championship.
Tracy Wilcox/The Gainesville Sun

team built around a senior that has been kick-started by freshmen.

Tim Tebow scored one touchdown and picked up 39 yards. He threw for a touchdown. But it was Leak who was the Most Valuable Player, managing the game beautifully and passing for 213 yards.

It was Percy Harvin who scored once and had 82 all-purpose yards. But it was Dallas Baker who scored the first touchdown.

You could point to the loss of Ted Ginn Jr. as a reason why Ohio State looked like the University of Phoenix, the online university that bought the naming rights to this stadium. Or you could point to the long layoff.

But when you saw what Florida did offensively, you hit your knees to give thanks to the layoff the Gators had to deal with.

We have seen in the past what Meyer does with extra days, an extra week. This break between games was longer than some mar-

riages and Meyer used it to refine his offense and add a few wrinkles for the first half.

He lined Cornelius Ingram up as a true, hand-on-the-ground tight end. He had Tim Tebow run a dip-and-sprint and find Andre Caldwell open for a score.

But mostly, these were the plays we'd seen before. This just wasn't the offense we'd seen before.

But it was a very familiar defense.

It made a Heisman Trophy winner from Ohio State look like Kirk Herbstreit. Today. Smith was firing balls into the ground and into the stands when he wasn't getting planted into the new turf at the stadium by Florida defenders.

And if we thought that was a buried myth about SEC speed being greater than Big 10 speed, well, when your defensive ends are faster than the other team's mobile quarterback, it's more of a fact now than a supposition.

"It ain't disrespect (for Ohio State), it's the truth," said wide receiver Andre Caldwell.

The way it started was perfect, to be honest. Meyer talked in his final pre-game press conference about how his team had been socked in the mouth so many times and that he admired the way they had come back each time.

On this glorious night, the punch in the mouth came on the first play when Ginn ran the opening kickoff back for a score.

But these Gators spit out the blood, bowed up and played an incredibly impressive game.

It was amazing. And now, Meyer can truly call this a great team.

And we can call him a great coach. ◣

The Gators huddle around coach Stan Drayton following their convincing win over Ohio State for the national championship. *Tracy Wilcox/The Gainesville Sun*

2006 Florida Statistics

(as of January 9, 2007)

TEAM STATS

Score by Quarters

Team	1st	2nd	3rd	4th	Total
Florida	90	150	83	93	416
Opponents	47	39	42	61	189

Category	Florida	Opp.
Scoring	416	189
Points Per Game	29.7	13.5
First Downs	285	216
Rushing	117	81
Passing	152	114
Penalty	16	21
Rushing Yardage	2,240	1,015
Yards Gained Rushing	2,567	1,384
Yards Lost Rushing	327	369
Rushing Attempts	476	370
Average Per Rush	4.7	2.7
Average Per Game	160.0	72.5
TDs Rushing	24	8
Passing Yardage	3,305	2,561
Att-Comp-Int	399-255-14	458-244-21
Average Per Pass	8.3	5.6
Average Per Catch	13.0	10.5
Average Per Game	236.1	182.9
TDs Passing	29	10
Total Offensive Yardage	5,545	3,576
Total Plays	875	828
Average Per Play	6.3	4.3
Average Per Game	396.1	255.4
Kick Returns: #-Yards	26-455	61-1,181
Punt Returns: #-Yards	49-499	19-71
Int Returns: #-Yards	21-150	14-117
Kick Return Average	17.5	19.4
Punt Return Average	10.2	3.7
Int Return Average	7.1	8.4
Punts-Yards	55-2,244	77-2,904
Average Per Punt	40.8	37.7
Net Punt Average	37.7	30.2
Penalties-Yards	116-888	81-595
Average Per Game	63.4	42.5
Time of Possession/Game	31:08	28:49
3rd-Down Conversions	74/167	61/186
3rd-Down Pct	44%	33%
4th-Down Conversions	9/18	6/18
4th-Down Pct	50%	33%
Fumbles-Lost	25-10	21-8
Sacks By-Yards	34-258	23-166
Misc Yards	23	0
Touchdowns Scored	57	23
Field Goals-Attempts	6-15	10-19
PAT-Attempts	50-54	19-20
Attendance	632,866	316,000
Games/Avg Per Game	7/90,409	4/79,000
Neutral Site Games	3/77,525	

INDIVIDUAL OFFENSIVE STATS

Rushing

Player	GP	Att	Gain	Loss	Net	Avg	TD	Long	Avg/G
Wynn, D.	14	143	721	22	699	4.9	6	26	49.9
Tebow, T.	14	89	478	9	469	5.3	8	29	33.5
Harvin, P.	13	41	437	9	428	10.4	3	67	32.9
Moore, K.	14	54	289	7	282	5.2	2	28	20.1
Fayson, J.	13	14	126	0	126	9.0	1	27	9.7
Caldwell, A.	14	21	126	24	102	4.9	1	27	7.3
Williams, M.	8	13	101	0	101	7.8	0	25	12.6
Leak, C.	14	77	238	208	30	0.4	3	45	2.1
Cornelius, J.	14	4	27	7	20	5.0	0	17	1.4
Manson, M.	12	4	17	2	15	3.8	0	9	1.2
Rowley, B.	14	1	3	0	3	3.0	0	3	0.2
James, B.	13	3	4	3	1	0.3	0	4	0.1
Higgins, T.	1	1	0	0	0	0.0	0	0	0.0
Wilbur, E.	13	1	0	2	-2	-2.0	0	0	-0.2
Team	8	10	0	34	-34	-3.4	0	0	-4.2
Total	14	476	2,567	327	2,240	4.7	24	67	160.0
Opponents	14	370	1,384	369	1,015	2.7	8	35	72.5

Passing

Player	GP	Effic	Cmp-Att-Int	Pct	Yards	TD	Long	Avg/G
Leak, C.	14	144.94	232-365-13	63.6	2,942	23	66	210.1
Tebow, T.	14	201.73	22-33-1	66.7	358	5	55	25.6
Caldwell, A.	14	472.00	1-1-0	100.0	5	1	5	0.4
Total	14	150.46	255-399-14	63.9	3,305	29	66	236.1
Opponents	14	98.28	244-458-21	53.3	2,561	10	48	182.9

Receiving

Player	GP	No.	Yards	Avg	TD	Long	Avg/G
Baker, D.	14	60	920	15.3	10	33	65.7
Caldwell, A.	14	57	577	10.1	6	66	41.2
Cornelius, J.	14	34	523	15.4	3	34	37.4
Harvin, P.	13	34	427	12.6	2	58	32.8
Ingram, C.	14	30	380	12.7	1	38	27.1
Moore, K.	14	8	58	7.2	1	16	4.1
Casey, T.	14	6	58	9.7	2	22	4.1
Wynn, D.	14	6	58	9.7	0	15	4.1
Nelson, D.	4	5	76	15.2	0	23	19.0
Cooper, R.	13	4	92	23.0	3	55	7.1
Tookes, K.	13	4	55	13.8	0	20	4.2
Latsko, B.	14	4	38	9.5	0	18	2.7
Murphy, L.	12	2	42	21.0	1	35	3.5
Fayson, J.	13	1	1	1.0	0	9	0.1
Total	14	255	3,305	13.0	29	66	236.1
Opponents	14	244	2,561	10.5	10	48	182.9

Interceptions

Player	No.	Yds	Avg	TD	Long
Smith, R.	8	44	5.5	0	29
Nelson, R.	6	70	11.7	1	70
Lewis, R.	4	35	8.8	0	35
Joiner, T.	2	0	0.0	0	0
McCollum, T.	1	1	1.0	0	1
Total	21	150	7.1	1	70
Opponents	14	117	8.4	1	40

Punt Returns

Player	No.	Yds	Avg	TD	Long
James, B.	33	363	11.0	1	77
Nelson, R.	12	93	7.8	0	21
Fayson, J.	3	30	10.0	0	16
Smith, R.	1	13	13.0	0	0
Total	49	499	10.2	1	77
Opponents	19	71	3.7	1	15

Fumble Returns

Player	No.	Yds	Avg	TD	Long
Harvey, D.	1	9	9.0	0	9
McDonald, R.	1	9	9.0	1	9
Pierre-Louis, W.	0	0	0.0	1	0
Total	2	18	9.0	2	9
Opponents	3	92	30.7	2	50

Kick Returns

Player	No.	Yds	Avg	TD	Long
James, B.	21	383	18.2	0	38
Moore, K.	4	63	15.8	0	26
Cornelius, J.	1	9	9.0	0	9
Total	26	455	17.5	0	38
Opponents	61	1,181	19.4	1	93

Scoring

Player	TD	FGs	Kick	Rush	Rcv	Pass	DXP	Saf	Pts
Hetland, C.	0	6-15	43-45	0-0	0	0-0	0	0	61
Baker, D.	10	0-0	0-0	0-0	0	0-0	0	0	60
Tebow, T.	8	0-0	0-0	0-0	0	0-0	0	0	48
Caldwell, A.	7	0-0	0-0	0-0	0	0-0	0	0	42
Wynn, D.	6	0-0	0-0	0-0	0	0-0	0	0	36
Harvin, P.	5	0-0	0-0	0-0	0	0-0	0	0	30
Leak, C.	3	0-0	0-0	0-0	0	0-0	0	0	18
Cornelius, J.	3	0-0	0-0	0-0	0	0-0	0	0	18
Moore, K.	3	0-0	0-0	0-0	0	0-0	0	0	18
Cooper, R.	3	0-0	0-0	0-0	0	0-0	0	0	18
Casey, T.	2	0-0	0-0	0-0	1	0-0	0	0	14
Ingram, C.	1	0-0	0-0	0-0	0	0-0	0	0	6
Fayson, J.	1	0-0	0-0	0-0	0	0-0	0	0	6
James, B.	1	0-0	0-0	0-0	0	0-0	0	0	6
Nelson, R.	1	0-0	0-0	0-0	0	0-0	0	0	6
McDonald, R.	1	0-0	0-0	0-0	0	0-0	0	0	6
Pierre-Louis, W.	1	0-0	0-0	0-0	0	0-0	0	0	6
Murphy, L.	1	0-0	0-0	0-0	0	0-0	0	0	6
Phillips, J.	0	0-0	5-5	0-0	0	0-0	0	0	5
Nappy, E.	0	0-0	2-4	0-0	0	0-0	0	0	2
Joiner, T.	0	0-0	0-0	0-0	0	0-0	0	1	2
McCollum, J.	0	0-0	0-0	0-0	0	0-0	0	1	2
Wilbur, E.	0	0-0	0-0	0-0	0	0-2	0	0	0
Rowley, B.	0	0-0	0-0	0-0	0	1-1	0	0	0
Total	57	6-15	50-54	0-0	1	1-3	0	2	416
Opponents	23	10-19	19-20	0-0	0	0-2	0	1	189

Total Offense

Player	G	Plays	Rush	Pass	Total	Avg/G
Leak, C.	14	442	30	2,942	2,972	212.3
Tebow, T.	14	122	469	358	827	59.1
Wynn, D.	14	143	699	0	699	49.9
Harvin, P.	13	41	428	0	428	32.9
Moore, K.	14	54	282	0	282	20.1
Fayson, J.	13	14	126	0	126	9.7
Caldwell, A.	14	22	102	5	107	7.6
Williams, M.	8	13	101	0	101	12.6
Cornelius, J.	14	4	20	0	20	1.4
Manson, M.	12	4	15	0	15	1.2
Rowley, B.	14	1	3	0	3	0.2
James, B.	13	3	1	0	1	0.1
Wilbur, E.	13	1	-2	0	-2	-0.2
Team	8	10	-34	0	-34	-4.2
Total	14	875	2,240	3,305	5,545	396.1
Opponents	14	828	1,015	2,561	3,576	225.4

Field Goals

Player	FGM-FGA	Pct	01-19	20-29	30-39	40-49	50-99	Lg	Blkd
Hetland, C.	6-15	40.0	0-0	3-3	1-7	2-4	0-1	42	0

Punting

Player	No.	Yds	Avg	Long	TB	FC	I20	Blkd
Wilbur, E.	53	2,244	42.3	64	5	12	22	1
Team	2	0	0.0	0	0	0	0	1
Total	55	2,244	40.8	64	5	12	22	2
Opponents	77	2,904	37.7	60	4	9	11	5

All Purpose

Player	G	Rush	Rec	PR	KOR	IR	Tot	Avg/G
Baker, D.	14	0	920	0	0	0	920	65.7
Harvin, P.	13	428	427	0	0	0	855	65.8
Wynn, D.	14	699	58	0	0	0	757	54.1
James, B.	13	1	0	363	383	0	747	57.5
Caldwell, A.	14	102	577	0	0	0	679	48.5
Cornelius, J.	14	20	523	0	9	0	552	39.4
Tebow, T.	14	469	0	0	0	0	469	33.5
Moore, K.	14	282	58	0	63	0	403	28.8
Ingram, C.	14	0	380	0	0	0	380	27.1
Nelson, R.	14	0	0	93	0	70	163	11.6
Fayson, J.	13	126	1	30	0	0	157	12.1
Williams, M.	8	101	0	0	0	0	101	12.6
Cooper, R.	13	0	92	0	0	0	92	7.1
Nelson, D.	4	0	76	0	0	0	76	19.0
Casey, T.	14	0	58	0	0	0	58	4.1
Smith, R.	14	0	0	13	0	44	57	4.1
Tookes, K.	13	0	55	0	0	0	55	4.2
Murphy, L.	12	0	42	0	0	0	42	3.5
Latsko, B.	14	0	38	0	0	0	38	2.7
Lewis, R.	14	0	0	0	0	35	35	2.5
Leak, C.	14	30	0	0	0	0	30	2.1
Manson, M.	12	15	0	0	0	0	15	1.2
Rowley, B.	14	3	0	0	0	0	3	0.2
McCollum, T.	14	0	0	0	0	1	1	0.1
Wilbur, E.	13	-2	0	0	0	0	-2	-0.2
Team	8	-34	0	0	0	0	-34	-4.2
Total	14	2,240	3,305	499	455	150	6,649	474.9
Opponents	14	1,015	2,561	71	1,181	117	4,945	353.2

INDIVIDUAL DEFENSIVE STATS

Player	GP	Solo	Ast	Total	TFL-Yds	No-Yds	Int-Yds	BrUp	Rcv-Yds
		---Tackles---			-Sacks-				-Fmbls-
Everett, E.	13	50	35	85	6.0-11	1.0-5	-	2	-
Siler, B.	13	50	27	77	10.0-40	3.0-21	-	3	1-0
Joiner, T.	14	31	28	59	4.5-9	-	2-0	6	-
Moss, J.	13	42	14	56	11.0-68	7.5-60	-	4	-
Smith, R.	14	43	11	54	3.5-11	-	8-44	8	-
Nelson, R.	14	34	17	51	2.0-6	-	6-70	5	1-0
McDonald, R.	14	19	17	36	4.5-10	3.0-15	-	5	1-9
Harvey, D.	14	24	11	35	13.0-95	11.0-89	-	-	3-9
Crum, B.	14	13	18	31	3.0-7	0.5-4	-	1	-
Lewis, R.	14	18	9	27	1.5-3	-	4-35	6	-
McCollum, T.	14	16	10	26	-	-	1-1	1	-
Cohen, J.	14	10	16	26	2.0-11	0.5-8	-	1	-
Thomas, M.	5	13	13	26	5.5-32	4.0-31	-	1	-
Doe, D.	14	14	8	22	1.0-1	-	-	-	-
Munroe, D.	14	11	5	16	1.0-2	-	-	-	-
Spikes, B.	9	9	6	15	1.0-2	-	-	2	-
Harris, S.	13	6	9	15	4.5-17	1.5-11	-	2	-
Brooks, N.	14	8	5	13	-	-	-	-	-
Jackson, K.	14	7	4	11	-	-	-	-	-
Smith, J.	14	5	3	8	-	-	-	-	-
Anderson, M.	13	7	1	8	-	-	-	1	-
McCollum, J.	13	4	4	8	-	-	-	-	-

Player	GP	Solo	Ast	Total	TFL-Yds	No-Yds	Int-Yds	BrUp	Rcv-Yds
		---Tackles---			-Sacks-				-Fmbls-
Pierre-Louis	12	3	4	7	-	-	-	-	1-0
Estopinan	6	1	4	5	-	-	-	-	-
Antwine, B.	8	1	3	4	-	-	-	1	-
Curtis, J.	6	2	2	4	-	-	-	1	-
Stamper, R.	2	3	1	4	1.0-2	-	-	-	-
Cooper, R.	13	2	2	4	-	-	-	-	-
Blackett, R.	10	3	1	4	-	-	-	-	-
Robinson, D.	13	2	1	3	1.0-1	-	-	-	-
Alford, L.	10	3	-	3	2.0-9	1.0-6	-	-	1-0
Murphy, L.	12	3	-	3	-	-	-	-	-
Phillips, J.	4	1	1	2	-	-	-	-	-
Williams, M.	8	-	2	2	-	-	-	-	-
Fritze, A.	3	2	-	2	-	-	-	-	-
Ijjas, J.	12	1	1	2	-	-	-	-	-
Cunningham	7	2	-	2	-	-	-	-	-
McMillan, C.	14	1	1	2	1.0-8	1.0-8	-	-	-
Team	8	-	1	1	-	-	-	-	-
Miller, D.	14	1	-	1	-	-	-	-	-
Gresham, D.	1	-	1	1	-	-	-	-	-
Leak, C.	14	1	-	1	-	-	-	-	-
Brewer, C.	1	1	-	1	-	-	-	-	-
Fayson, J.	13	1	-	1	-	-	-	-	-
Rissler, S.	14	1	-	1	-	-	-	-	-
Harvin, P.	13	1	-	1	-	-	-	-	-
Baker, D.	14	1	-	1	-	-	-	-	-
Total	14	472	295	767	79-351	34-258	21-150	50	8-18
Opponents	14	558	280	838	71-284	23-166	14-117	37	10-92

Acknowledgments

The entire staff of *The Gainesville Sun* contributed to the coverage of the 2006 University of Florida football national championship season. The photography, design, graphics and sports departments did the great bulk of the work.

SPORTS DEPARTMENT

Sports editor: Arnold Feliciano
Assistant sports editor: Jeff Barlis
Lead sports designers: Missi Koenigsberg, Larry Savage
Copy editor: Adam West
Columnists: Pat Dooley, Hubert Mizell
Reporters: Robbie Andreu, Kevin Brockway, John Patton, Brandon Zimmerman
Sports assistants: Talal Elmasry, Jon McDonald, Daniel Shanks, Ray FitzGerald

PHOTOGRAPHY DEPARTMENT

Director of photography: Brian W. Kratzer
Assistant director of photography: Rob C. Witzel
Photographers: Doug Finger, Tracy Wilcox, Aaron Daye, Alexander Cohn
Photo lab assistant: Morgan Petroski

DESIGN

Design editor: Rob Mack
Design assistant: Troy Griggs

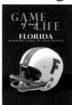